# SEXISM:
# Scientific Debates

Edited by
CLARICE STASZ STOLL
Sonoma State College

ADDISON-WESLEY PUBLISHING COMPANY
Reading, Massachusetts
Palo Alto, California
London • Don Mills, Ontario

To my parents,
Clarence and Mary,
who didn't think the difference
worth the fuss

This book is in the
Addison-Wesley Series in
Dialogues in the Social Sciences

Consulting Editor
Marcello Truzzi

 Printed in the United States of America. Published simultaneously in Canada. Library of Congress Catalog Card No. 72-11077.

DO

# Preface

This book is about gender and society – about what the labels "female" and "male" mean for the individual so labeled and his role within the social organization. It presents the reader with possible reasons for sex distinctions, considers what effects these distinctions have on the individual and society, and determines whether and how the situation can be changed.

Since this anthology deals with the sociology of sex roles, it must, by necessity, come to grips with the concept of sexism. Sex stratification systems exist in virtually every area of life, throughout time and across cultures – and in all societies the male rules as the dominant figure. However, in spite of the pervasiveness of this social stratification, it can no longer be taken for granted as a constant of social life. Yet most social scientists have accepted it as immutable fact even though many women and men today question the validity of this principle of social organization and look to the social scientist and other scholars for information and direction.

In compiling this volume my aim was to meet the following needs:

1. Although women activists often make use of arguments found in scholarly articles for their political ends, the original sources rarely appear in the political literature published by the women's movement or in volumes about the movement. This set of readings is therefore designed to complement the popular writings by exposing the reader to some of the original source material.

2. Although several collections of scholarly articles on women exist, they are organized along traditional disciplinary lines and hence stop short of the political implications of the scientific findings. Today's readers are dissatisfied with this rather antiseptic, sterile presentation of social science data. After all, men and women are part of the social universe which is being studied by the social scientists.

I have therefore chosen readings that reflect the variety of questions social scientists have raised as well as suggest a wide range of possible solutions to the problem of eliminating sexism. The selections thus contain a number of different viewpoints, raising (and sometimes answering) such questions as:

To what extent can we say that sex roles are rooted in biology or early conditions?

Is it possible to identify fairly universal "masculine" and "feminine" behaviors, traits, or tendencies?

Are the differences between sex roles decreasing?

Is androgyny (the disappearance of sex distinctions) the answer to breaking down the sex stratification system, or must some differences remain?

Given one's beliefs on these matters, what are the policies or laws (or changes in both) that will implement these beliefs?

How can one reconcile policies favoring "individual freedom" with those favoring the "general welfare" of the society?

Can science and scholarship help us resolve this dilemma?

How does the fact of sexism in scholarship confound our search for solutions?

In compiling these selections, I wished to include as many theoretical viewpoints and types of research design as possible. The choice was at times difficult. Several of my favorites had to be omitted to avoid repetition of a particular standpoint or style of research (and as anyone who has edited an anthology will readily understand, permission problems may also account for what would seem like an obvious omission). The overall balance satisfies me, and I will stand on my final choice. There are review articles, arguments based on available data, survey results, government statistics, and an experimental study. Some writers are aware of sexist bias and others aren't. Some make policy suggestions while others cry

"No, sexism is fiction!" As my opening essay should make clear, no one of the papers can unequivocally be labeled as either "sexist" or "feminist." This anthology is not another reader on women's liberation, nor is it a set of statements by women who identify with the movement. (However, you will find some rhetoric in these pages though it is hidden in the folds of scholarly language.) Except for the Introduction, the sequence in which the selections appear or will be read is immaterial, for each provides some insights into the others.

The publications in the Dialogues in the Social Sciences series are to be brief, yet thorough enough to treat important issues in depth. In order to present arguments in detail and with little editing, I therefore chose to include only a small number of selections. I believe that writers should be allowed to speak for themselves, so that the readers face few of those ellipses which leave mysterious and often important gaps. To supplement each writer's own bibliography, I have added a list of suggested readings that either expand on or dispute the work at hand.

Most of you neither are nor plan to be professional social scientists. Nonetheless I hope that this volume will encourage you to go beyond the data and arguments presented here to develop a critical attitude toward social science literature as well as more thoughtfully reasoned political views about sex roles and society — whatever your final position on these matters may be.

My first debt in preparing this anthology is to all those women at Sonoma State College who asked me to help with the Woman's Studies program. Special thanks go to J. J. Wilson, my (female) colleague in English, who has introduced me to the topic of women in literature and encouraged my interdisciplinary outlook on sex roles. Several others supported me while commenting critically on parts of the text, including Mildred Dykeman, Saul Geiser, Peter Manning, and Marcello Truzzi. I shared the routine tasks of manuscript preparation with Barbara Paige, for she is too talented to be given all the tedium of that job.

I have no wife to thank. My family, which consists of Kendra, assorted animals, and the fictive kinship of friends, did not suffer because of my labors on this text. It would be patronizing to suggest otherwise, for all are too busy defining themselves through themselves.

*Petaluma, California*
*September 1972*

*C. S. S.*

# Contents

# Introduction

To edit a book on "sexism" is in a way a mark of a genuine revolution in social experience, for the word cannot be found in dictionaries of the late 60's. Yet, with its companion epithets of "male chauvinist" and "sexist," it has become commonplace in the language. Although the word was coined only recently, its root and meaning are clear. It defines a society's discriminatory ideologies and practices as they are reflected in the opportunities given to individuals for self-expression, with sex being the basis for selective acceptance or rejection. Like the term racism, it was coined by those who question that the dominant group's—in this case male—standards, values, goals and strategies are the best, if not the only worthwhile ones, for members of a society.

Obviously it would be historical naiveté to date interest in sexism with the origin of the word. Writings, speeches, and groups attacking sex discrimination go back two centuries in American society, beginning perhaps with Abigail Adams, who reminded her husband that the rights of the female sex should be remembered in the Constitution. They were not, and throughout the 1900's courageous women such as Elizabeth Cody Stanton, the Grimke sisters, Susan B. Anthony, Harriet Tubman, and many others unmentioned in most history books worked for the political suffrage that did not come until 1920. (For historical material on the feminist movement, see Sinclair, 1965; Flexner, 1971; Lloyd 1971; Tanner, 1971.)

During the four decades following the suffrage amendment, women in general showed little concern with their rights. However, as more women entered the labor market and found themselves assigned to jobs that in most cases did not do justice to their educational level and training, their dissatisfaction and frustration grew. Then, in 1964, the federal Civil Rights Act, prohibiting sex discrimination in employment, provided women with a political weapon, and the blacks' civil rights movement showed them how to publicize grievances dramatically and firmly. The second wave of the women's rights movement was set in motion.

The movement's impact cannot be gauged by the reports in TV, radio, or newspapers which tend to focus on its most sensational manifestations. However, some evidence of its force can be observed in the changing content of the popular women's magazines (*Ladies Home Journal, McCall's, Redbook, Good Housekeeping,* etc.) which, during the 60's, gradually moved from housekeeping and romantic fiction to articles reflecting a wider range of feminine interests and responsibilities. Once taboo topics, such as abortion information, divorce counseling, and career planning, now appear side by side with recipes, fashion, and decorating tips. Journalists and editors no longer presume that because the law offers equal opportunities to women in many areas, these opportunities do, in fact, exist. Readers are encouraged to speak out and act upon their grievances to ensure that the intent of the laws becomes reality. Nevertheless, many women active in the rights movement belittle these changes because the editorial content continues to be surrounded by advertising that is generally sexist in assumption.

Feminists point out that the special interest magazines and newspapers written and edited by the women themselves–not by some mass media organization–reflect more accurately the changes that are occurring. These publications, for example, *Women: A Journal of Liberation, Notes From the Second Year, Aphra, Women's Liberation, Ms,* and numerous local newspapers, contain personal accounts of discriminatory experiences, political statements, practical advice on how to organize for change–what one would expect from any group attempting to solidify its cause. The most striking aspect of these publications is the diversity of opinion expressed in them. *Perhaps the only statement a group of women discussing liberation agree upon is that they are "oppressed."* Just what this oppression is and how it is to be overcome is the basis of considerable debate. Some women want company-run day care centers while others vehemently oppose this idea as only another device to trap women into less desirable jobs. Some want to separate their lives totally from men, which need not imply a preference for lesbianism, while others seek ways to draw men into the movement. Some want the legal institution of marriage abolished. Others care primarily for "equal pay-equal work" and do not mind the marriage contract as currently defined. Accordingly, a variety of organizations have sprung up, ranging from the largely professional National Organization for Women to the loose radical coalition known as the Redstockings.

Women's challenges of public policy attack every institution in society: the family, the economy, the political order, education, religion, and leisure. Disagreements among the women themselves can be traced back to the paradoxes inherent in the U.S. Constitution, which directs the government to provide for the general welfare while individuals are to pursue happiness (Bernard, 1971). The first directive argues for the optimum utilization of resources available to society. Proponents of this view would argue for policies that would make more effective use of women in the occupational market in the spirit of "what's good for the country is good for the women." The second directive suggests a policy which would encourage individual human fulfillment. Proponents of this position would advocate changes that would expand women's choices on a more profound level—go beyond the removal of job discrimination barriers by giving men and women equal property rights and by providing equal sharing of child care in the spirit of "what's good for the women is good for the country."

In general, it has been easier to implement the first directive in our society because the policy of general welfare is readily couched in the statistics and language compatible with (masculine-dominated) bureaucratic and technocratic thinking. To illustrate, women can point to the shortage of doctors along with the apparent discrimination against women in medical schools and draw up any number of proposals to encourage women into medicine and thereby decrease the shortage. Those who argue for the pursuit-of-happiness position introduce dilemmas of choice into such proposals that are not settled by statistical compilations. They might raise questions such as: Should women be encouraged to take up a profession that seems organized more for self-interests than for the general health care of the community? How can we assure that women doctors will not be directed toward the less desirable and lower-paying areas of medicine? What good is the education of women doctors if the organization of medical practice does not accommodate those women—and men—who wish to be active in child-rearing? These are some of the questions that generate discussion among women who hold similar overall goals.

## SEXISM AND SCIENTIFIC SCHOLARSHIP

As described so far, sexism is an ideology with a rhetoric of social grievances as its counterpoint. Public policy is ultimately a matter of making decisions based on value judgments. What does science have to do with values and social movements?

Most obviously, the social sciences can help us analyze the development of women's rights movements and perhaps provide a basis for predicting its future course. Economics can provide data on the labor situation of women. Psychology can elucidate the special characteristics and talents of women. In fact, researchers in these disciplines are carrying out investigations along these lines.

Furthermore, most people trust that science has something to say with regard to policy, and many women have used scientific data as evidence that their ideology is based upon "fact." Economic data demonstrate the large discrepancies in income of comparably trained males and females. Numerous child development studies chart the sex-based differential shaping of expectations of success. Research on the physiology of sex has illuminated the biologically exceptional sexuality of the human female. Not all research supports the women's cause—as they see it. For example, feminists tend to discredit any research that suggests a natural basis for sex differences.

It is to be expected that a technological society such as ours will use science as a persuasive device and scientific evidence as justification for its laws and directives issued by the administrative, legislative, or judicial branches. This is most strikingly illustrated by the Supreme Court's explicit reference to social science research as a rationale for making its revolutionary school desegregation decision in 1954. No doubt this decision is a further reason for women to look to science for support.

Another factor in our acceptance of science as a persuasive force is its "objectivity." Personal documents allow the reader to ask, "How can you be so sure that discrimination is the cause of your dissatisfactions with life?" The eloquent biography of a woman who describes her struggles against apparent oppression may arouse a reader's sympathy but won't necessarily establish the fact of oppression itself. However, many of us will accept scientific data with little dispute because we expect them to be based on large numbers of cases reduced by statistics to concise summary statements. Scientific methods are public and reproducible; we can test the reasoning at various stages and even attempt to replicate the results. Finally, science is considered to be above ideological disputes and its results are therefore to be more trustworthy—or so this seems.

In reality our assumptions about science and the scientific method are likely true only in the long run, but do not hold for any one study, or discipline, or line of research. Scientific activities are social activities, and the results of scientific research reflect the social purposes of the actors as well as the explicit knowledge-seeking aims. Many investigators will admit that personal reasons motivate their choice of research topics. For example, much of the research on school desegregation is performed by social scientists who admit to a personal commitment to this educational policy. Consequently, the social implications of their research may gain a momentum that exceeds the explicit value judgments of the individual scientist such that an entire discipline may support a view of the world that is inherently antiracist, or supertechnological, or Puritan, or whatever.

*There is growing evidence that the social sciences are sexist;* this should not be surprising given that white males predominate in virtually every scientific profession. In addition, these males run the professional societies, are overrepresented on editorial boards and granting agencies, and therefore become public figures. (Ask yourself who, in a field of interest you know best, are the leading intellectuals: you will likely list all men.) These men have shared a socialization process and set of experiences quite different in many respects from those experienced by females. Consequently, they are likely to perpetuate certain attitudes toward the world that are based on sexist assumptions. Female scientists learn this tradition and may unwittingly perpetuate it.

The first apparent evidence of sexism in scholarship is the very paucity of research on women or on sex differences. Very few women are mentioned in history books. (*His*tory is just that, feminists will tell you, not *her*story.) Economics has traditionally ignored woman as a serious contributor to the economy because much of her work is not recompensed financially and her participation in the labor force is considered to be surplus. As for sociology, I discovered that most books in my personal library did not even mention that there are two sexes. Sociology speaks mainly of the society of men. These examples can probably be repeated with every scholarly discipline.

What happens when man and woman are objects of study? The example of psychology, as analyzed by Weisstein (1969), may apply to other disciplines as well. Weisstein reviewed some of the major theoretical ideas of women's nature as stated by the field's most eminent (male) scholars. The general view presented was that woman is nurturant, is happiest being so, and contributes most to society by remaining so. These views continue to be found in professional writings even though they lack empirical data or documentation.

In addition, empirical studies of sex differences often suffer a serious methodological flaw, namely, that the researchers do not "blind" the observations. That is, when they interpret personality tests or study biographies they know which cases are male and which are female. Although any standard text on research practices urges the scientist to avoid this approach, many personality researchers still fail to blind their analysis. Much of our "knowledge" of sex differences comes from these poor studies.

Weisstein also reported how, following participation in an intensive graduate seminar on sex differences, almost all the students failed to sort out a pile of unlabeled clinical tests into "male" and "female." This, she suggests, is additional evidence that what psychology has to tell us about sex differences is probably wrong.

Sexism permeates scholarship in yet other ways. Several analyses of research on marriage and the family (Heiskanen, 1971; Bernard, 1972) have indicated that white male middle-class values permeate the studies and the conclusions drawn from them. For example, high divorce rates are presumed to reflect a failure of marriage and are unhealthy for the society. Very few studies deal with working wives, unwed mothers, house husbands, nonmarital sex, or even housewifery itself. In studies of sexual behavior, concepts such as love, intimacy, violence, aggression, power, that are relevant to an understanding of sexuality are overlooked, while "numbers of orgasms" or "varieties of sexual positions used" are counted (Stoll, 1972). The emphasis on the latter may seem natural to men who have been raised in American society, but it does not appear so to a woman. No wonder that we have not gone far in our understanding of sexuality beyond establishing norms of sexual performance to silently compare ourselves against.

If scientific scholarship is not free of sexist bias, can it be useful as a tool for studying sexism as a phenomenon and for designing public policy? I argue that it does, provided one approaches the scholarly literature critically, recognizing that a writer has some ideological position on sexism, however unstated. By "position" I mean more than "for" or "against"–it includes attitudes concerning sex oppression, its reasons, and what lines of social policy seem to be indicated to remedy the situation. A critical reader will also be aware of rules of evidence and examine arguments closely for definition of terms, soundness of logic, and possible alternative interpretations of data. *Scientific scholarship does not prove anything; at best it demonstrates the plausibility that some things are true rather than others.*

## HOW TO TELL A MAN FROM A WOMAN

Before turning to the selections, a major assumption of this book must be examined: Are there two sexes that can be differentiated? What does it mean to say that one part of society is "female," the other "male"? The answer is not a simple one.

We all know that men and women differ in their external genitalia. Rather we take this to be true, for in addition to (1) "normals," there are (2) hermaphrodites, who have the external appearances of both sexes, and (3) individuals whose external sex organs do not permit a definite assignment to either sex. How do we identify these latter two cases? By reproductive capacity? But a segment of each will be sterile. Glandular criteria such as testicles or ovaries again result in one-both-none categories. A comparison of hormonal output–estrogenic (female) vs. androgenic (male)–might lead us to assign people who look and act like one sex to the other.

Chromosomal identification, perhaps? This procedure is used by the World Olympic Games to ensure that "men" are not competing in women's events. A cell scraping from the mouth can be examined for the presence of either the XX (female) or the XY (male) chromosomal combination. Although the general acceptance of this test seems to bear out its validity, it is actually open to debate, because there exist X, XXX, XYY, XXY anomalies which are usually accompanied by other abnormalities of sexual physiology. And in some cases it has been found that an individual has a Y chromosome in some cells though not in others (Money, 1969; Chapter 5).

These variations and abnormalities in sexual physiology suggest that the distinction between male and female is not clear-cut. Not only does each measure of sex fail to sort all individuals into two categories, but there is always the possibility that different tests may assign one and the same person to both sexes. How, then, are we able in our everyday life to categorize individuals as male or female with such ease? Money, Hampson, and Hampson (1955) studied 76 ambisexual or hermaphroditic individuals and found that *the best predictor of adult sex role is not physiology.* What mattered more than external appearance, hormones, gonads, or chromosomes was the assignment of sex at birth. They found further that whenever a person designated to one sex at birth was reassigned to another in later years, the chances of successful change decreased beyond the first few years of life. Thus sexual identity appears to be socially defined, and its major qualities are imprinted on the child at a quite early age. Some researchers use the term *gender identity* to emphasize that sexual distinctions are socially rather than physiologically determined.

Of course, sexual physiology is not the only criterion available if we wish to separate people into two sex groupings. We lack any large-scale surveys of the population along lines of sex physiology, but it seems likely that most of us who identify with one sex would score as belonging to that sex if all the various physiological measures were used. Clinical studies of rare varieties of humans should not dissuade us from thinking that two sexes are natural. Consider the fact of secondary sex characteristics. Males in any culture can be identified by larger stature, beard growth, narrow hips, straight extremities, tendency toward baldness, and many other physical features. These are "normal" for men in general though not necessarily for any one man. There are hirsute women and wide-hipped men. The average American woman is taller than the average man in some other cultures. Incidentally, this illustration supports the thesis that some secondary sex characteristics are not "natural" in the sense of being typical of humans in general, but may reflect generations of breeding according to certain norms of attractiveness within a culture.

Because most "normal" men and women differ from each other in physiological characteristics, a "nature versus nurture" controversy is implied in all studies on sex roles. As will be shown here, there are data demonstrating that the central nervous system and hormonal output of men and women differ so as to affect general behavioral dispositions. On the other hand, some argue that these differences can be explained by socialization, for after all upon birth every infant is immediately identified as male or female by the choice of name (and blanket color). Most scholars do not adopt one of these viewpoints to the exclusion of the other—there simply is not sufficient evidence to reach a definitive answer. Furthermore, many assume that it is unreasonable to expect that *either* biology *or* society is all. Not surprisingly, some feminist sympathizers discount the effect of biology on behavior, since its acceptance might imply that existing sex roles in society are predetermined and immutable.

The fact that there are physiological differences between the sexes is also reflected in some of the dilemmas public policy confronts when it tries to wrestle with charges of sexism. The typical man's body makes use of leverage in a manner different from the woman's. Most machinery is designed for the male leverage system, and men occupy the jobs in which these machines are used. No one inspects men to see whether in fact they have a male leverage system, yet women are barred from performance because "obviously" their bodies will be inadequate. Do we now design a new set of machines so that most women can use them? Or do we give both men and women strength and leverage tests, perhaps firing unsuitable men who have held these jobs in the past?

This illustration also shows how the existence of typical sex characteristics, whether genuine or mythical, simplifies life for social decision-makers, be they two persons approaching a closed doorway at the same moment or a labor planner in government. In even trivial cases (such as the problem of converting machinery to make it suitable for use by women) a decision in favor of conversion raises complex problems of economy and technology.

Society views men and women as different, and the consequences are all too apparent. Nonetheless, different societies vary in their *sexual dimorphism*, i. e., the different norms they apply to and expectations they have of males and females. Most of the distinctions turn out to be cultural (see Seward and Williamson, 1970). For example, American men are raised to compete and be successful, are given opportunities to succeed and may actually do so. In the Middle East men are permitted to be emotional and are so, while their wives are stolid and practical. While physiology of sexual differences may have some universal elements, the content of sex roles or gender identities does not. From some of the selections we shall find that sexual dimorphism in American society may be on the decrease. What would it mean if sex roles were eliminated and androgyny prevailed—a goal some feminists espouse? The answers being offered are, we shall see, quite different.

## A NOTE ON THE READINGS

The selections here document the extent of sexism in our society, along with various theoretical interpretations of why it exists. Several articles look to the meaning for society and for individuals of changes in sex role definitions. I chose these selections to sample the range of approaches to the topic, and have tried to highlight the possible conflicts and debates in my introductions. I have also attempted to select from among the most forceful and scientifically competent representatives of a particular viewpoint. There are no strawmen here—though this does not mean that the articles necessarily are infallible or definitive statements.

Because the study of sex differences is a recent one and also because of its political nature, most of the arguments presented here build a careful case for one or two main ideas. In doing so the writers might have overlooked or ignored information that does not quite fit their schemes. So much effort is spent in constructing an elegant argument that other equally plausible explanations are passed by. These very human failings are one reason for not relying on one study or theory in itself when developing your own ideas about sexism.

A series of questions are debated throughout these papers, either explicitly or implicitly. The major ones are:

1. *On Masculinity And Femininity:* Can we say that males and females are different beyond the reproductive or sexual sphere? If there are differences, are they rooted in biology or society? What does it matter if there are differences that are fairly universal?

2. *On Sexism In Society:* Are there some universally sexist forms of social organization? What are the reasons for sexism? Can all sexist patterns be changed? What policies are needed to change the system of discrimination? Is androgyny (the elimination of sex role differences) the answer?

3. *On Science As A Guide:* How can we utilize the results of scientific scholarship when it itself is biased by sexist ideologies? Can science help us with policy decisions?

Given that sexism does pervade the scholarly work, you should not expect outlandishly radical ideas here—except indirectly. A few papers were written for specialized audiences and thus may not seem relevant at first glance. They all are though, and the comments that introduce each selection will give you some idea as to the value of the material. At the very least you will learn something about sexism and its effects on you and society.

Two important sets of information are omitted from this anthology. First, there is no material on the woman's movement itself. Considerable literature, some of which is cited above, is available to the reader interested in this topic. (See also Kanowitz, 1969; Adams and Briscoe, 1971; Reeves, 1971.) Second, there are no articles dealing with human sexuality and its relation to sex roles. I believe that the sexual basis of sexism is of major importance. Hence I regret that space limitations prevented me from including relevant material, such as the provocative, if polemical, contributions made by Norman Mailer (1971) and Germaine Greer (1971) or the research of Masters and Johnson [as summarized by Brecher and Brecher (1966) or Fromme (1970)].

With these limitations in mind, let us begin. . .

## REFERENCES

Elsie Adams and Mary Louise Briscoe (editors), *Up Against the Wall, Mother. . .* , Beverly Hills, Ca.: Glencoe, 1971.

Jessie Bernard, *The Future of Marriage*, New York: World, 1972.

Jessie Bernard, *Women and Public Policy*, Chicago: Aldine, 1971.

Ruth and Edward Brecher, *An Analysis of Human Sexual Response*, New York: Signet, 1966.

Germaine Greer, *The Female Eunuch*, London: Paladin, 1971.

Veronica Stolte Heiskanen, "The Myth of the Middle-Class Family in American Family Sociology," *American Sociologist*, **6** (1971): 14-18.

Leo Kanowitz, *Women and the Law*, Albuquerque, N. M.: Univ. of New Mexico, 1969.

Trevor Lloyd, *Suffragettes International*, New York: American Heritage, 1971.

Norman Mailer, *The Prisoner of Sex*, New York: Signet, 1971.

John Money, "Sex Reassignment as Related to Hermaphroditism and Transsexualism," pp. 91-113 in Richard Green and John Money, editors, *Transsexualism and Sex Reassignment*, Baltimore: Johns Hopkins Press, 1969.

John Money, Joan G. Hampson, and John L. Hampson, "An Examination of Some Basic Sexual Concepts: The Evidence of Human Hermaphroditism," *Bull. of the Johns Hopkins Hospital*, **97** (1955): 301-319.

Nancy Reeves, *Womankind*, Chicago: Aldine-Atherton, 1971.

Georgene H. Seward and Robert C. Williamson (editors), *Sex Roles in Changing Society*, New York: Random House, 1970.

Andrew Sinclair, *The Emancipation of the American Woman,* New York: Harper, 1965.

Clarice Stasz Stoll, "The Sociology of Sex Roles: Essay Review," *The Sociological Quarterly* 13 (1972), 419-425.

Leslie B. Tanner (editor), *Voices from Women's Liberation,* New York: Signet, 1971.

Naomi Weisstein, "Kinder, Küche, and Kirche as Scientific Law," *Motive,* 29 (1969): 78-85.

## SUGGESTED READINGS

Toni Cade (editor), *The Black Woman,* New York: New American Library, 1970. Poems, stories, and essays by contemporary women who suffer the additional stigma of being racially oppressed.

Elaine Morgan, *The Descent of Woman,* New York: Stein and Day, 1972. Challenges the traditional theories for the evolution of sex differences, which usually center on the needs of men, by explaining them in terms of the needs of women in early evolution.

Robin Morgan (editor), *Sisterhood is Powerful,* New York; Vintage, 1970. The most comprehensive collection of writings from the recent woman's movement in America.

Miriam Schneir (editor), *Feminism,* New York: Vintage, 1972. The essential historical writings, including speeches, essays, and fiction by prominent feminists, female *and* male.

# Developmental Differentiation of Femininity and Masculinity Compared

John Money

John Money should receive the acclaim in the study of sexism that Kinsey or Masters and Johnson have received in the study of sexuality. Though a psychologist by training, he has penetrated into the area where pediatrics, endocrinology, genetics, and sexual behavior overlap. He was a major figure in the development of the Gender Identity Clinic at Johns Hopkins Hospital, a unit that assists in the therapy of individuals with uncertain sexual identity, i.e. hermaphrodites and transsexuals (individuals who feel they have been born the "wrong" sex and undergo surgical reversal).

Most of Money's writings, which are addressed to medical researchers, are relevant to the scientific study of sexism in that he provides data on individuals who have changed their sex for various reasons. The contribution here aptly summarizes for lay audiences the implications of his work. On the other hand, Money discusses cases of individuals who have been born with an uncertain sexual identity, a fact that suggests a biological continuum of male-female, yet later he identifies known correlates of "male" and

---



The author is supported in research by a USPHS Research Career Development Award, no. MH-K3-18,635. Research drawn on for this paper was done under Grant no. M-1557, the National Institute of Mental Health, The U. S. Public Health Service; and under an earlier grant from the Josiah Macy, Jr., Foundation.

"female" in our society. The contradiction is resolved by remembering that Money uses "masculine" and "feminine" to mean societally assigned gender identity, not a variable that can be differentiated by any physical measurement.

Money argues that some psychosexual differences appear to be learned, while others "go deeper," perhaps originating in the endocrine and nervous systems. Do you agree with his interpretations in each case? How strong is the evidence? Were any findings new for you? How does the new information influence your previous ideas about the nature of sex differences?

Money takes a mass of data on the differences between females and males and relates them to physiology or early conditioning. Take each one in turn, e. g. mortality rates, perceptual differences, etc., and consider whether this theory is reasonable in every instance. What sense can you make of the differences if Money's theory appears shaky?

---

The simple dichotomy of innate versus acquired is conceptually outdated in analysis of the developmental differentiation of femininity and masculinity, which is not to say that one should obliterate the distinction between genetics and environment. Rather, one needs the concept of a genetic norm of reaction that defines limits within which genetics may interact with environment and vice versa, of an environmental norm of reaction that defines limits within which environment may interact with genetics. Then one would speak of a norm of interaction when genetics and environment are in conjunction under optimal circumstances. Abnormality, or deviation from the norm of interaction, may be engendered by alteration of either a genetic or an environmental factor to be other than optimal.

In the sexual differentiation of the human embryo, the norm is ordinarily male when the sex chromosomes are X and Y, and female when they are a pair of X's. Nonetheless, in some lower species, the environment of the chromosomes may be so manipulated experimentally as to reverse the norm. In amphibian experiments, complete reversal of phenotypic sex has been achieved. Thus, an egg of the Mexican Salamander, or axolotl, fertilized as a genetic female can be forced to develop as a morphologic and fertile male, under the influence of an embryonic testicular graft. This phenotypic male, which is genotypically female, is then capable of mating with a regular female. The only tell-tale sign of their both being genetic females is in the faulty sex ratio of the offspring: 25 per cent of the offspring that should have been males are females with an abnormal sex-chromosome complement (25 per cent of the offspring are genetically normal males, 50 per cent normal females, and 25 per cent abnormally homozygous females [Humphrey, quoted in Jones and Scott, 1958, p. 17]).

In human beings, complete phenotypic reversal of genotypic sex is not known either experimentally or in spontaneous occurrence; but in the phenomena of hermaphroditism there are some quite remarkable partial reversals of incongruities of differentiation. Striking incongruity is found in the female-simulant type of male hermaphroditism known as the syndrome of testicular feminization. In this condition, a baby is born who is morphologically a normal female in appearance and who eventually matures spontaneously into a perfectly normal feminine puberty except for the absence of menstruation. There is no uterus from which to menstruate. The tubes and ovaries are lacking. The internal structures which are present are paradoxically male. The two gonads, one in each groin, are microscopically testicular, but they secrete estrogen lavishly. They are sterile. The chromosome count is 46, XY, as normally expected for the male. Psychosexually these people invariably develop as feminine.

Cases of the testicular feminizing syndrome illustrate a fundamental principle of embryonic sexual differentiation, namely, that irrespective of the sex chromosomes, the norm of reaction in the absence of gonads is to differentiate as a morphologic female, unless a masculinizing principle is added. Jost, In France, proved this point with exceptional clarity (Jost, chap. 2 in Jones and Scott, 1958).

Jost succeeded with the very delicate task of castrating fetal rabbits *in utero* without fatally interrupting pregnancy. If castrated early enough, namely, before the twenty-first day, all the fetuses differentiated as females, internally and externally. No more than three days later, on the twenty-fourth fetal day, castration did not interfere with the proper continuance of masculine differentiation already begun. On the twenty-third day, castration arrested masculine differentiation and resulted in incompletion of the masculine organs, so that they looked hermaphroditically ambiguous.

It was possible to reverse the effects of castration by implanting testosterone pellets where the gonads had been. An implant on one side only has a specific localized action, producing lateral hermaphroditism, that is, masculine internal differentiation on one side and feminine on the other. Lateral hermaphroditism some times occurs spontaneously in human beings.

Jost's demonstration appears to be but one example of a broadly applicable principle of female precedence. Nature herself apparently takes cognizance of the greater hazard of being a male and prepares for the greater mortality of the male by decreeing that more male babies will be born than female.

The sex ratio of births is 106 males to 100 females (Stern, 1960, chap. 21). Though not absolute, this birth ratio holds widely in countries where accurate birth statistics are kept. The ratio of male to female conceptions has not, for obvious reasons, been ascertained, but sex-chromatin surveys of early abortions have yielded findings of male-female abortus ratios of 160:100 (Tricomi, Serr, and Solish, 1960) and of 122:100 (Szontágh, Jakobovits, and Méhes, 1961).

The initial surplus of males at birth is progressively diminished by a higher death rate for males. It is higher at all ages (Figure 1), even when female vulnerability is enhanced by the mortality of the childbearing period. With variations dependent on local conditions, males still outnumber females during the marrying

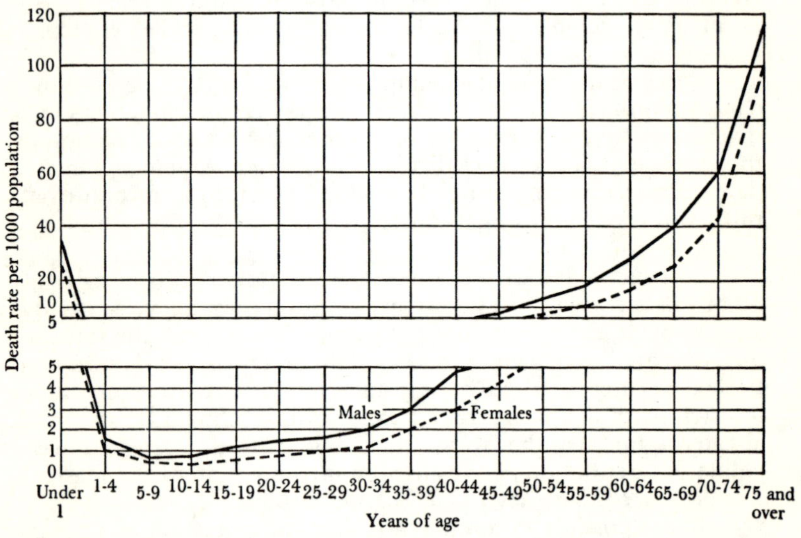


**Figure 1.** Mortality rates of white males and females, United States, 1950. From *Principles of Human Genetics,* 2nd ed., by Curt Stern, San Francisco: W. H. Freeman and Company, 1960. (Data from U.S. Department of Health, Education, and Welfare.)

ages. Numerical equality of the sexes is reached around the age of fifty. Thereafter the males die off more rapidly—leaving a sellers' market for geriatric male escort service!

The greater vulnerability of the male shows up in more than mortality tables. There are diseases also to which the male is more prone. Those of special interest here are the psychosexual and sex-behavioral pathologies. Inevitably, the epidemiology of sex pathologies is not accurately known, owing to the population's legal and moral fears of self-incrimination in disclosing personal data. It is part of the clinical lore of psychiatry and sexology that male far exceeds female incidence of the more rare sexual anomalies, especially those in which erotic arousal becomes linked visually to some incongruous or incomplete object or image. Kinsey, Pomeroy, Martin, and Gebhard (1953, chap. 16) reviewed relevant data on exhibitionism, peeping and voyeurism, fetishism and transvestism, as well as other nonpathological preferences in visual stimulation.

The Kinsey surveys furnish incidence figures which show an excess of male over female with respect to both homosexual and animal contacts (Kinsey, Pomeroy, Martin, and Gebhard, 1953, chaps. 11 and 12; Kinsey, Pomeroy, and Martin, 1948, chaps. 21 and 22).

The figures for homosexuality are as follows: the accumulative incidences of overt contacts to the point of orgasm in the female sample reached 13 per cent, whereas in the males the figure was 37 per cent. Further, it was estimated that 4 per cent of white males are exclusively homosexual throughout life, whereas the corresponding figure for females is only a half to one-third as many. A similar ratio of 8 men to 3.6 women was found in the accumulative percentages for animal contacts. For the majority of individuals, contacts with animals were sporadic and transient; exact figures are missing, but men outnumbered women in repeating the experience and in becoming habituated for a period of years.

There is no ready explanation of why psychosexual differentiation as a male may, like embryonic differentiation, be more complex and open to error than differentiation as a female. It is necessary to know a great deal more about the entire process of psychosexual differentiation. One inroad into this problem has been made by the study of human hermaphrodites (Money, Hampson and Hampson, 1955; Money, Hampson, and Hampson, 1957; Hampson and Hampson, 1961; Money, 1961b; Money, 1962).

In the annals of hermaphroditism and the related congenital sexual deformity of penile agenesis, it has happened that individuals of the same anatomical and physiological diagnosis have been raised, some as girls, some as boys. The appropriate surgical corrections are undertaken, and at teenage the congruous hormonal therapy is given. Then it is usual to discover that the gender role and psychosexual identity agree with the sex of assignment and rearing. The importance of these cases is that they show a complete overriding of sex-chromosomal constitution and of gonadal status in the establishment of gender role and identity.

There are other cases that demonstrate the ascendancy of assigned sex over hormonal sex also, notably female hermaphrodites with the adrenogenital syndrome raised and living as women. Before the advent of cortisone therapy in 1950, to suppress adrenal androgens, these women were exceptionally heavily virilized and totally lacking in female secondary sexual characteristics. The subordination of their hormonal sex to their assigned sex in psychosexual differentiation is, therefore, all the more remarkable.

Unquestionably, it is difficult to establish and maintain a feminine gender role and erotic identity when the body is heavily virilized, and harder still if the sexual organs are hermaphroditically masculinized with gross enlargement of the clitoris and partial fusion of the labia as in a scrotum (or homologously vice versa, for boys). Yet even this contradiction in external genital appearance, surprisingly enough, can be tolerated and a feminine identity established at variance with it.

Hermaphroditically ambiguous external genitals may, however, tell a lie to their owner, as well as to other people, so that it is therapeutically highly desirable to have them surgically corrected at an early age. The internal organs, by contrast, being hidden, do not appear to have any effect on the differentiation of gender role and identity.

The evidence of hermaphroditism, then, shows that it is possible for psychosexual differentiation to be contradictory of chromosomal sex, gonadal sex, hormonal sex, external genital sex, and internal genital sex, and to agree instead with assigned sex.

One is confronted with the conclusion, perhaps surprising to some, that there is no primary genetic or other innate mechanism to preordain the masculinity or femininity of psychosexual differentiation. Factors of innate origin may exert influence as secondary determinants, however. The obvious example is the anatomy of the external genitalia which, in the normal course of embryonic events, is determined by biochemical organizer substances which in turn are regulated by chromosomal sex. Postnatally, the anatomy of the genitals determines the sex of assignment, the gender-specific reactions of other people to the growing child, and the proof to the child through his own body image that other people are correct.

In psychosexual differentiation, the analogy is with language. Genetics and innate determinants ordain only that language can develop and differentiate, provided that the sensory and motor capacities are intact and that communicational stimulation is adequate, but not whether the language will be Nahuatl, Arabic, English, or any other. Psychosexually, also, genetics and innate determinants ordain only that a gender role and identity shall differentiate, without directly dictating whether the direction shall be male or female. In fact, the expected norm of reaction may be completely reversed by factors that come into play after birth.

As gender role and identity become fully differentiated, they become permanently indelible and imprinted, and subsequently as irreversible and powerful in influencing behavior as if innately preordained *in toto*. This idea of the indelibility of the products of the interaction of heredity with experience and learning is rather novel in psychology, but profoundly important. The evidence from hermaphroditic cases of sex reassignment is that the critical period for gender imprinting is in early childhood, beginning with the onset of mastery of language. The die is cast, pretty well, by the age of six, after which major realignment of gender role and identity is rare.

It is not for a moment claimed that psychosexual differentiation as male or female is a simple-minded matter of environmental determinism. Rather, the environment is viewed as an integral and essential constituent of that differentiation, more profoundly contributory than has often been allowed.

Nonetheless, for all the psychosexual differences that can be regarded as environmentally conditioned, in the sense of culturally learned, there are some psychosexual differences that go deeper. Their roots lie, obscure still to the scientific gaze, apparently in the endocrine and nervous systems.

It is an unsolved question as to whether some sex-different hormonal factory may, by originally affecting the organization of the nervous system itself, eventually affect sex-different behavior. Phoenix, Goy, Gerall, and Young (1959) ventured such a hypothesis after studying the behavior of female guinea pigs some of which had been rendered visibly hermaphroditic, others not, by injecting the pregnant mother with androgen. The guinea pigs exposed to androgen *in utero* subsequently exhibited, in a complex series of tests, mating behavior which, though not absent in normal females, had an arousal threshold and frequency of occurrence approaching that of the normal male. The behavior was not sex specific; rather, its threshold and frequency was.

Irrespective of neuroanatomy and fetal androgens, it is quite possible that the sex hormones, represented in different ratios in the two sexes, have different threshold effects on the nervous system, both receptor and effector. Smell acuity, for example, at least for some compounds, appears to be regulated by estrogen level. Women generally have greater acuity than men. Though Elsberg, Brewer, and Levy (1936) reported three cases to the contrary, acuity is at its peak for most women when they are not in their progesterone (menstruating) phase of the menstrual cycle (Schneider and Wolf, 1955). Their acuity is lost after ovariectomy, but regained if they are given estrogen (Le Magnen, 1952). Hypophysectomy, which suppresses ovarian function, also brings about loss of the sense of smell (Schon, 1958).

Another sex difference that appears to be hormonally regulated is the intensity or urgency of libido, or sexual desire. In this case, there is considerable evidence that androgen is the libido hormone for both men and women (Money, 1961a, c). When men are given estrogen, as in the treatment of prostatic cancer, they usually report loss of sexual desire and of potency. Excessive androgens of adrenal origin in women with the adrenogenital syndrome are accompanied usually by a low threshold for erotic arousal and for clitoral tumescence, both of which are somewhat increased when androgen is suppressed by cortisone therapy. Normal women deprived of their normal adrenal androgens by either adrenalectomy or hypophysectomy, as part of the treatment of breast cancer also experienced a lessening or total loss of libido, which was not the case when they were deprived only of estrogens by ovariectomy (Wexenberg, Drellich, and Sutherland, 1959; Schon and Sutherland, 1960). Conversely, normal women given androgen treatment for various gynecological reasons many times find their libidinal intensity increased, perhaps to unfamiliarly high levels. The androgens of eroticism in normal, untreated women may be of adrenal origin or may derive from the closely related progestins. They may also be exogenous. A typist of one of my recent manuscripts disclosed that young men about town who wish to put the make on their young women have learned to spike the girl friend's Martini with testosterone one weekend in advance.

Closely connected with libidinal threshold is yet another sex difference, namely, in responsiveness to visual and pictorial images and to erotic narrative material. Men, in general, are much more responsive to this type of stimulation than are women, and they are responsive in a different way. For example, the strip-tease girl at a show or the pin-up girl on a calendar becomes the object of a male's desire. If these same stimuli arouse a women, as they often do, it is because she projects herself into the position of the seductive one. Then, significantly enough, her desire is not for anyone and everyone in the admiring herd but for the one special person, even though he may be many miles absent, who is the object of her long-term romantic affection.

The other side of the woman's coin is that it is rare for her to be erotically aroused—romantically alerted, yes, but not erotically aroused—by the perceptual or pictorial image of a male. For the male, the other side of the coin is that, unless he be homosexual, he will not be able to project himself into the image of another male on erotic display. Thus, in exhibitions and stag movies of sex and copulation, a male is quite likely to be more aroused by the reiteration of the female image when two women are shown in Lesbian play than when a man and a woman are shown together. Herein may lie an element of the explanation of why, in man-made laws, male homosexuality is a crime and Lesbianism is unmentioned.

It can, of course, be argued that these perceptual-arousal differences between men and women are culturally determined and perpetuated—there are no sex shows, commercially, for women. The counter argument is that culture is built on biology which it may never totally defy. It is anecdotal evidence, but nonetheless pertinent, that women who have, in my professional experience, reported a capacity to be aroused to erotic action by sexy pictures of men or by narrative erotic material have been women who have or once had elevated androgen levels secondary to the adrenogenital syndrome. The significant thing, be it noted, in these cases, is that masculinism applies only to the level of arousal threshold, not its content. The arousing image was heterosexual and perfectly appropriate for a woman. Thus, hormonal influences may have the power to regulate erotic threshold, but apparently not erotic content.

To explain what determines the content of the image that will have erotic arousal power, one turns to the concept of imprinting as discovered and expanded by the school of animal ethologists. In imprinting theory, one postulates an innate releasing mechanism (IRM) in the nervous sytem. An IRM requires a perceptual stimulus to trigger it into action. The physical dimensions—color, size, shape, shading, contour—of the stimulus may vary, but only within limits phylogenetically determined. Thus, a parakeet may get imprinted to make love to another bird, to a wobbly celluloid toy, or to a human finger. A phylogenetically acceptable stimulus presented at the critical time in the life cycle becomes imprinted rather easily and then possesses a remarkable quality of persistence and preeminence over competitor stimuli. Imprinting could account for the remarkable specificity and persistence of the most preferred and most potent type of erotic stimulus, in both healthy and abnormal psychosexual functioning. Imprinting, in fact, is a way of explaining the very existence of aberrancy in psychosexual imagery and perceptual arousal.

Perception plays a part in another sex difference, namely, in relation to distractibility. More than the female, the male is in his erotic pursuits fairly promiscuously distracted from one love object to another, especially over a period of time, except perhaps when he is in the vortex of having just fallen desperately in love. The female is more steadfastly tied to a single romantic object or concept. In the act of copulation, by contrast, it is the male who has a singleness of purpose, perhaps oblivious even to noxious stimuli, and likely to be unable to continue if successfully distracted by a competing stimulus. This sex difference appears to hold widely in the animal kingdom (Beach, 1947, p. 264). Horsley Gantt (1949, p. 37), director of the well-known Pavlovian Laboratories at Johns Hopkins, wrote:

> A marked difference between the male and female cat is that the female's interest in food is not inhibited by the sexual excitation of copulation, for she, as well as a bitch, will accept food not only after coitus but even during the act! . . . The female is however much more strongly oriented about the offspring than about the sexual act, she undergoes a great inhibition of conditional reflexes and of some unconditional reflexes postpartum, a fact which has been demonstrated several times in my laboratory with dogs.

The male's ready arousal by perceiving a new erotic stimulus perhaps relates to his greater expenditure of energy in the service of sexual searching, pursuit, and consummation. Expenditure extends also to adventurous, exploratory roaming, to assertiveness and aggression, and to the defence of territorial rights. Of course the male does not have exclusive prerogative, in these respects, but there does indeed seem to be a sex difference in the frequency with which these patterns of energy expenditure are manifest.

The difference becomes apparent even in childhood. When boys are out staking territory claims, constructing hideouts, forts, or camps, and fending off rival intruder gangs, girls are expending somewhat less energy, usually closer to home, making lairs and homes for the young and raising doll babies.

A striking demonstration of the sex difference, during childhood, in types and variety of energy expenditure is provided by the figures for accidental deaths in children. Table 1 compares statistics for males and females, under and over four years of age, in the United States and in Venezuela, for five principal types of

**Table 1** Accidental deaths in children according to the five principal types in the continental United States, 1956, and in Venezuela, 1954, by sex and age group*

| | Continental United States | | Venezuela | |
|---|---|---|---|---|
| Type of accident | Males | Females | Males | Females |
| | | 1-4 years | | |
| Motor vehicle | 800 | 638 | 28 | 22 |
| Drowning | 463 | 191 | 47 | 38 |
| Fire and explosion of combustible material | 443 | 472 | – | – |
| Poisonings, solid or liquid | 196 | 140 | 28 | 19 |
| Falls | 155 | 99 | – | 7 |
| Burns | – | – | 26 | 27 |
| Poisonous bites by venomous animals | – | – | 6 | – |
| | | 5-14 years | | |
| Motor vehicle | 1,785 | 855 | 44 | 28 |
| Drowning | 981 | 204 | 55 | 15 |
| Firearms | 357 | 72 | – | – |
| Fire and explosion of combustible material | 263 | 404 | – | – |
| Falls | 138 | 50 | 19 | 4 |
| Poisonous bites by venomous animals | – | – | 39 | 6 |
| Burns | – | – | 15 | 31 |

* Reproduced from Goddard (1959), courtesy of Public Health Reports.

accident. Inspection of the table shows that the deaths of boys exceeded those of girls chiefly in those situations in which the boys had gotten in harm's way or had inaugurated some dangerous activity. In brief, the boys went further to meet death than the girls did.

Evidence to supplement the various findings on the human species may be found in the observations of Harlow (1962) on the macaque monkey during childhood. Harlow found that male monkey children make many more threats toward other monkeys, boys or girls, than do female monkey children, whose threats, moreover, are reserved primarily for other girls. The young females retreat more often than the males, specifically by adopting the female sexual posture. The male youngsters initiate more play contacts, with playmates of either sex, than do female. In addition, rough-and-tumble play is strictly for the boys! With increasing age, male infants show increasing frequency of the male mounting position in their copulatory play. The males show practically no grooming behavior which, in adults, is specifically feminine sexual behavior.

It would be going too far, on the basis of this kind of evidence, to equate masculinity with aggressiveness and femininity with passivity, as has sometimes been fashionable. It is rather that the sexes differ with regard to the types of behavior pattern that they initiate and persist in, versus those that they discontinue most frequently.

It is not possible, in the present state of knowledge, to relate the foregoing types of male-female difference in patterns of energy expenditure and sexual play either to genetic mechanisms, to fetal hormonal effects on the central nervous system, or to hormonal functioning in childhood. Harlow's own studies do show, however, that proper exercise of patterns of energy expenditure in childhood play are essential to the final emergence of adult sexual patterns. Monkeys, male and female, raised in individual cages and deprived of play with their agemates failed to develop normal sexual behavior and were hopelessly unable to master the art of copulation even under the tutelage of a cooperative, experienced mate.

Parenthetically, one may raise the question of whether the suppression, in our own human society, of childhood sexual play may adversely affect sexual behavior in adulthood and perhaps promote the occurrence of sexual aberration.

A few of Harlow's female monkeys did, he reports, after heroic efforts of animal husbandry, become pregnant. They had known no real, live monkey mothers of their own, since they had been raised in individual cages with experimental surrogate objects for mothers. When they had their own babies, they were totally inept at motherhood—as liable to crush and kill their babies on the floor as to pick them up gently.

Motherhood itself, then, is yet another instance of behavior in which genetic patterns and environmental patterns in interaction with one another are equally important to the mature coordination and emergence of the final product.

My wheel has done a full turn, all the way from X and Y chromosomes to motherhood. I close with a witticism attributed to Oscar Wilde on the occasion of his being asked to explain the difference between the sexes. He paused epigrammatically and replied: "Madam, I can't conceive."

## REFERENCES

Beach, F. A. 1947. A review of physiological and psychological studies of sexual behavior in mammals. *Physiological Reviews,* 27:240-307.

Elsberg, C. A., Brewer, E. D., and Levy, I. 1936. The sense of smell. IV. Concerning conditions which may temporarily alter normal olfactory acuity. *Bulletin of the Neurological Institute of New York,* 4:31-34.

Gantt, W. H. 1949. Psychosexuality in animals. In *Psychosexual Development in Health and Disease* (P. H. Hoch and J. Zubin, eds). New York, Grune & Stratton.

Goddard, J. L. 1959. Accident prevention in childhood. *Public Health Reports,* 74:523-534.

Hampson, J. L., and Hampson, J. G. 1961. The ontogenesis of sexual behavior in man. Ch. 23 in *Sex and Internal Secretions* (3rd ed., W. C. Young, ed.). Baltimore, Williams & Wilkins.

Harlow, H. F. 1962. The heterosexual affectional system in monkeys. *American Psychologist,* 17:1-9.

Jones, H. W., Jr., and Scott, W. W. 1958. *Hermaphroditism, Genital Anomalies and Related Endocrine Disorders.* Baltimore, Williams & Wilkins.

Kinsey, A. C., Pomeroy, W. B., and Martin, C. E. 1948. *Sexual Behavior in the Human Male.* Philadelphia, Saunders.

Kinsey, A. C., Pomeroy, W. B., Martin, C. E., and Gebhard, P. H. 1953. *Sexual Behavior in the Human Female.* Philadelphia, Saunders.

LeMagnen, J. 1952. Les phénomènes olfactosexuels chez l'homme. *Archives des Sciences Physiologiques,* 6:125-160.

Money, J. 1961a. Components of eroticism in man: 1. The hormones in relation to sexual morphology and sexual desire. *Journal of Nervous and Mental Disease,* 132:239-248.

Money, J. 1961b. Hermaphroditism. In *The Encyclopedia of Sexual Behavior* (Albert Ellis and Albert Abarbanel, eds.). New York, Hawthorn.

Money, J. 1961c. Sex hormones and other variables in human eroticism. Ch. 22 in *Sex and Internal Secretions* (3rd ed., W. C. Young, ed.). Baltimore, Williams & Wilkins.

Money, J. 1962. Cytogenetic and psychosexual incongruities with a note on spaceform blindness. *American Journal of Psychiatry.*

Money, J., Hampson, J. G., and Hampson, J. L. 1955. An examination of some basic sexual concepts: The evidence of human hermaphroditism. *Bulletin of The Johns Hopkins Hospital,* 97: 301-319.

Money, J., Hampson, J. G., and Hampson, J. L. 1957. Imprinting and the establishment of gender role. *Archives of Neurology and Psychiatry,* 77:333-336.

Phoenix, C. H., Goy, R. W., Gerall, A. A., and Young, W. C. 1959. Organizing action of prenatally administered testosterone propionate on the tissues mediating mating behavior in the female guinea pig. *Endocrinology,* 65:369-382.

Schneider, R. A., and Wolf, S. 1955. Olfactory perception thresholds for citral utilizing a new type olfactorium. *Journal of Applied Physiology,* 8:337-342.

Schon, M. 1958. Psychological effects of hypophysectomy in women with metastatic breast cancer. *Cancer,* 11:95-98.

Schon, M., and Sutherland, A. M. 1960. The role of hormones in human behavior. III. Changes in female sexuality after hypophysectomy. *Journal of Clinical Endocrinology and Metabolism,* 20: 833-841.

Stern, C. 1960. *Principles of Human Genetics.* 2nd edition. San Francisco, Freeman.

Szontágh, F. E., Jakobovits, A., and Mehes, Ch. 1961. Primary embryonal sex ratio in normal pregnancies determined by the nuclear chromatin. *Nature,* 192:476.

Tricomi, V., Serr, D., and Solish, G. 1960. The ratio of male to female embryos as determined by the sex chromatin. *American Journal of Obstetrics and Gynecology,* 79:504-509.

Waxenberg, S. E., Drellish, M. G., and Sutherland, A. M. 1959. The role of hormones in human behavior. I. Changes in female sexuality after adrenalectomy. *Journal of Clinical Endocrinology,* 19:193-202.

## SUGGESTED READINGS

Ruth Herschberger, *Adam's Rib,* New York: Harper and Row, 1970. A lucid re-interpretation of the biological data so often used to perpetuate sexist ideas.

Ashley Montagu, *The Natural Superiority of Women,* New York: Collier, 1970. Using much of the same data Money presents, Montagu argues for a change from hu-man to a humane society.

Robert Stoller, *Sex and Gender,* New York: Science House, 1968. A cautious, non-technical survey of research on sex and sexual identity, including cases of neuters, hermaphrodites, and transsexuals.

# Infant Sex Differences

Judith Bardwick

Judith Bardwick precedes the discussion included here with a review of the evidence supporting the hypothesis that the central nervous system of males and females exhibits differences. A variety of experiments on animals and man have demonstrated that the injection of opposite sex hormones leads to changes toward behaviors more characteristic of the opposite sex. For example, adult human females, upon receiving the male hormone testosterone, display an increase in activity level, aggressive behaviors, and sexual drive. Furthermore, there is some evidence of a stage in fetal development at which an "early and irreversible force of sexual-identity" is established. These ideas and phraseology may seem vague, but that is partly due to the fact that they represent unfamiliar conclusions derived from a new examination of the thesis that sex identity is biologically determined.

The selection begins as Bardwick continues to review personality research on sex differences during child development. It is noteworthy that little work has been done in this area — another instance of a scientific discipline ignoring a relevant variable, perhaps out of sexist bias of the scientists. Most of Bardwick's arguments reflect the view that culture shapes sex differences, although she does accept the likelihood of "innate" or con-

---

stitutional differences. She argues that one has to examine how the culture inhibits or enhances basic biological responses. In American society it appears that notions of masculinity do not match well with the natural physical and psychological development of males, a discrepancy reflected in the greater rate of psychopathology among males in later life. Bardwick then analyzes the phenomenon of transsexuality to emphasize further that sexual identity may have its origins in the fetal stage.

Both Bardwick and Money seem to argue that nurture builds on nature. What if physiological research provides further evidence that there are hormonal and central nervous system differences between men and women? What if males are "naturally" aggressive? What does this mean for those who value peace? Is aggression always destructive?

Consider the physiological research process itself. It is relatively easy to obtain valid measures of hormone levels, but how does one establish objective measures of "aggression" and "sex impulses"? Could it be that women score low on "aggression" because the measure used reflects a masculine definition of the term? In other words, women may be equally "aggressive" as men, but their everyday activities may not have been analyzed sufficiently to permit us to recognize the aggressive component. Maybe all that apparently solid physiological research has a sexist base. Maybe not. . . .

---

Endocrine research has led to the hypothesis of differences in the central nervous system of males and females. If such differences really exist, we should expect to find them clearly demonstrated in differences in the behaviors of male and female animals and children. Even before socialization, there ought to be measurable differences in the general behavioral dispositions of the two sexes.

I have been personally impressed with the basic and consistent personality differences between male and female infants and would like to be able to present a long list of infant researches that support this idea. This I cannot do for several reasons: Infant research is just beginning, and little of it has been directed towards sex differences. Most of the studies have used fewer than 40 infants and those infants were divided into male versus female, breast-fed versus bottle-fed, first-born versus infants with siblings—with the number of infants in each category extremely small. The length of gestation of each infant has been omitted, so we have no estimate of differences in maturity at birth. (Normal gestation time is from eight-and-a-half to nine-and-a-half months, which could well mean a significant difference.) An even more important reason, which should be obvious to anyone who handles infants, is that because infants lack control of their bodies they display a great deal of irrelevant and meaningless activity. This makes it difficult to validly interpret the infant's behavior, especially if the researcher is unfamiliar with that infant except for the testing hour. There is another equally important difficulty—the behavioral repertoire of the infant is very limited. This also makes interpretation difficult and reminds us that the behaviors we are especially interested in do not appear in recognizable and specific form until the infant is about six months old. Many of the studies have used infants just a few days old.

I therefore find especially interesting the longitudinal studies of children that have found consistent sex differences over a period of time in the dimensions of activity, passivity, introversion, and extroversion (Kagan and Moss, 1962; Schaefer and Bayley, 1963; Macfarlane, Allen, and Honzik, 1954; Murphy et al., 1962). Generally speaking, these studies find that the basic response to the environment is consistent from early childhood to adulthood, if the personality parameters are conceived in abstract terms and not in terms of age-specific behaviors. Females tend to be more passive, less active, more introverted. It seems most likely that only some of the personality variables will prove to be sex-linked, but in an ultimate sense, we may find that the sex-linked dimensions are broadly related to the reproductive functions of the two sexes.

If we look at other mammals, particularly other primates, we find that the sex differences are consistent with the findings for humans. Within a month after birth, male rhesus monkeys are wrestling, pushing, biting, and tugging while the female monkeys are beginning to act shy, turning their heads away when challenged to a fight by young males (Goy, 1968). Harlow (1962) has found that male macaque monkeys show a greater likelihood of making a threatening gesture in the face of attack and are less likely to withdraw from an attack. Jensen and Bobbitt (1968) also found that in the first few weeks of life the male monkeys develop behavior patterns quite different from the female monkeys. The males quickly surpass the females in the rate of achieving independence from their mothers (which was helped by the mothers punishing them more, paying less attention to them, and holding and carrying them less). The males had higher general activity levels, did more biting, hitting, pushing, shoving, yanking, grabbing, and jerking. They also did more thumbsucking and more manipulation of their genitals.

In 1962 Harlow observed that male monkeys threaten other males and females but that females do not threaten immature males. Females display a much higher incidence of passivity responses. "In all probability the withdrawal and passivity behavior of the female and the forceful behavior of the male gradually lead to the development of normal sex behaviors." Grooming patterns sharply differentiate the sexes: "Caressing is both a property and prerogative of the females." Play behavior in the playroom is seldom initiated by the females. Play involving body contact is far more frequent among the males and is almost invariably initiated by the males. "Real rough-and-tumble play is strictly for the boys."

Harlow went to a second-grade school picnic where he observed sex differences in human play that were very similar to the patterns he had seen in monkeys. "These secondary sex-behavior differences probably exist throughout the primate order, and moreover, they are innately determined biological differences regardless of any cultural overlap." Harlow concluded, "We believe that our data offer convincing evidence that sex behaviors differ in large part because of genetic factors."

We know that when girls enter school they are developmentally ahead of boys of the same age. Kagan and Lewis's observations (1965) seem pertinent:

> The data are persuasive in suggesting that girls display more sustained attention to visual stimulation, and prefer more novel auditory patterns than boys at both 6 and 13 months of age. The 6-month data suggested greater cardiac deceleration to the matrix of lights among girls, and longer fixation times to the film-presented pictures. Moreover, girls displayed greater attention to the novel music pattern at 6 months, whereas the boys preferred to listen to the simple repetitive tone.
>
> At 13 months of age, the girls sustained attention to the blinking lights across all 12 trials, whereas the boys showed rapid habituation. Finally, the girls' preference for more novel auditory patterns noted at 6 months was still present at one year of age. For girls showed greater cardiac deceleration than boys to the low-meaning–high-inflection paragraph,

> and it was argued that girls may have a preference for auditory inputs with greater stimulus uncertainty.
>
> If one assumes that sustained attention and a preference for deviation from the familiar are *mature* attentional habits, it appears that girls are developmentally advanced over boys as early as 6 months of age. These data support the general belief that there are basic biological differences between boys and girls in rate of psychological development during the opening years of life.

The differences we see in human infants that seem to be constitutional in origin are shown in Table 1. What I think generally happens is outlined in Table 2.

The girl is constitutionally less likely to gratify impulses in activity that the parents find offensive, such as aggression or masturbation. In addition, she is better able to make accurate assessments of the demands of people in the environment and to behave so as to minimize stress. She will, earlier than the boy, cope with discord verbally. As a result of her own behavior potentials there is less parental-cultural stress on girls to give up infantile behaviors. Dependency upon adults, which later forms part of the feminine role but which is part of the normal disposition of infants and young children, will be permitted. Because of the lack of external stress and the lack of internal impulses, she will develop fewer internal controls over impulses. She will have a more diffuse body image and a self-concept still linked, through dependency, to the evaluations of others. She will have a higher need for approval and acceptance, and a greater motoric passivity. The lack of internal ego controls and an independent concept of self leads to a dependent sense of self-esteem. This makes her more amenable to cultural patterning, to more conformist behavior, to better school achievement.

For boys, there is a greater and earlier cultural pressure not to act out impulses. There are few mothers who can tolerate impulsive physical activity that leads to continuous injury, to physical aggression that might injure siblings and playmates, or to public masturbation. In addition, at about the age of 2 to 2½, when children are clearly no longer infants, the dependency behaviors that were normal for both sexes are now seen as babyish or feminine in boys. Girls can be tomboys without undue notice; boys can never be sissies.

*Because the culture interprets infantile behavior as feminine, and because it rejects many of his early impulses, the boy is soon*

**Table 1** Sex differences in infancy and early childhood

| Boys | Girls |
| --- | --- |
| At Birth | |
| Larger size and weight (Terman and Tyler, 1954); more muscle mass (Garn, 1957, 1958) | Greater motoric passivity (Bell, 1960; Kop, 1946) |
| More activity | More sensitivity to stimuli; sensitivity to a greater number of stimuli |
| Correlation of low sensitivity with higher prone head reaction (Bell and Darling, 1965) | Greater tactile and pain sensitivity; higher skin conductance, greater irritability during an anthropometric examination (Bell and Costello, 1964; Lipsitt and Levy, 1959) |
| 6 Months | |
| Better fixation response to a helix pattern of lights | Longer fixation time to visual stimuli, less motoric activity, and greater cardiac deceleration (Lewis et al., 1963) |
| | Better fixation to a human face (Lewis, Kagan, and Kalafat, 1965) |
| | Greater responsiveness to a social stimuli; more social orientation (Bayley, 1964) |
| Greatest cardiac deceleration (a measure of attention) to an intermittent tone | Greater cardiac deceleration to complex jazz music (Kagan and Lewis, 1965) |
| 13 Months | |
| Maximum response to a verbal stimulus high in meaning and low in inflection | Maximum response to a verbal stimulus high in meaning and inflection; implies a response to a person (Kagan and Lewis, 1965) |
| Preference for low complexity stimuli | Preference for high complexity stimuli (Kagan and Lewis, 1965) |
| | Earlier language development, especially inflection |
| Possible better figure-ground differentiation | Greater field dependency; less likely to eliminate irrelevant stimuli, awareness of contextual relationships |

Table 2 Socialization of early sex differences

| Boys | Girls |
|---|---|
| **Testosterone** | |
| More physical activity | Less physical activity |
| Greater aggressiveness | Less aggressiveness |
| Less pain sensitivity | More pain sensitivity |
| More insistent sexual impulses | Lower sexual impulses |
| More masturbation | Less masturbation |
| **Figure Ground** | |
| More inclined to focus on figure as distinct from ground | More influenced by entire context |
| More likely to ignore what is irrelevant to problem being solved or to goal | More attention to complexity, to visual, aural, social stimuli |
| **Personality** | |
| More intent on own purposes, more likely to be unaware of or resistant to parental demands | More aware of social demands, better able to assess parental wishes and anticipate them |
| Receives more parental pressure to inhibit or channel aggressiveness; more likely to be rewarded for achievement, to have to struggle for sense of autonomy against parental pressure | More likely to conform, to be rewarded for goodness, to remain dependent on others for self-esteem |
| Higher self-esteem based on achievement | Higher self-esteem based on being loved |
| Independence, achievement, objectivity | Interdependence, conformity, subjectivity |

*pressured to conform to parental expectations in direct opposition to his predispositions. This necessitates an early development of internal ego controls. The boy who is considered excessively passive and withdrawing will be pushed to conform to an active masculine image, while the very active and aggressive boy will be pushed to conform to a less egocentric active style. The percentage of boys who are pushed to change their life-style is high, and the cost shows up in a higher evidence of male psychological pathology.*

To the young boy, the prohibiting parents can no longer be seen as a stable and undemanding source of self-esteem. As a result, slowly and with difficulties, with frequent outbursts of aggression, he gives up the parents as his primary source of self-esteem and develops a self-regard system relatively independent of the evaluations of others. His self-esteem is more likely to be based on his achievements, which are more likely to be objective and tangible. The girl's self-esteem is more likely to depend on her acceptance, which is personal and intangible. This is an extremely important difference between the sexes. The girl rarely achieves a sense of independent self-esteem until she is a young woman—if then. The difficulty of this process in the boy is attested to by the frequency of behavioral outbursts, the higher incidence of psychological pathology, and, perhaps most important, by the intrusion of emotion into his perceptual-cognitive spheres so that he does worse than the girl in school until about the fifth grade. It is as though he is too preoccupied with the development of his identity and with the control of his important and prohibited impulses.

The cultural pressure on boys, the reaction to their constitutional behavioral predispositions, is great. The cultural pressure on girls is much less, because their general predispositions and the cultural interpretation of what is acceptable are more nearly matched. The differences in impulses plus the greater perceptual-cognitive sophistication of the girl will enable her to experience a less stormy childhood. As a result she is cognitively mature, in an interpersonal and scholastic way, earlier than the boy. But emotionally, she leaves the relationships of childhood slowly, if at all.

I am suggesting, then, that children are born with personality characteristics that lead to behaviors, and that these behaviors are reacted to evaluatively by parents. The child with these behavior potentials is a member of a specific sex, and the behaviors are evaluated by what is acceptable for members of that sex. I would also suggest that most parents respond to the infantile quality of the child for the first 2 to 2½ years, and then significant sex-role discrimination increases as he or she comes to be seen as less of an infant and more of a child. The very early sex differences do not originate as a response to parental actions.

It is not, then, that children are born with a built-in set of responses that will determine their behaviors irrespective of environmental reactions. Nor is it true that children are "tabula rasa," or blank clay, destined to be molded solely by the imprint of a parental (and heavy) hand. Predispositions to respond and to perceive similar stimuli may be significantly different between the sexes because of genetically determined differences that have their roots in physiology. The endocrine data and the infant animal and human studies lead to the assumption of general behavioral tendencies that are sex linked and that may be related to the presence or absence of testosterone at a critical stage in development. The behaviors of the organism, whether animal or human, will be responded to, rewarded, punished, or ignored in the process of socialization. I suggest that most cultures may be reinforcing behavior tendencies or predispositions *characteristic* of the sexes. In that case these behavior tendencies would be so pervasive that we notice body contributions only in exceptional circumstances such as that of the transsexual.

## THE TRANSSEXUAL

Transsexuals know that they are trapped inside a body of the wrong sex. They have identified completely with the role of the opposite sex. Despising the genitals of their body, their single aim is to rid themselves of these disgusting parts and achieve through surgery and endocrine therapy the body of the opposite sex, which is their "true" sex. The transsexual is not a homosexual; the homosexual has the normal psychological investment in his own genitals. Moreover, the transsexual is, by and large, not mentally ill. He is able, excepting this syndrome, to function normally. It is important, however, to understand the intensity of emotion involved–autocastration by male transsexuals is not uncommon.

What is the origin for this extraordinary motive and conflict? Pauly (1965) reviewed the clinical material on 100 cases of male transsexuals and found that gonadal development was generally normal, that the steroid levels were within normal limits for those patients for whom information was available, and their secondary sex characteristic development was also within normal range. The absence of a clear physical pathology in the majority of transsexuals has been noted by many researchers.

Transsexuals appear in Greek mythology and in histories of ancient Greece and Rome; they have been described in many cultures around the world and throughout history (see Green, 1966). They are not found in any particular family constellation with consistency–although many patients are described as having an excessively loving and permissive (seductive?) mother and often a weak or absent father (Stoller, 1967; Hampson, 1961; Benjamin, 1966; Pauly, 1965), the frequency of this family constellation is too low to account for the frequency of the pathology. Of Benjamin's 152 male patients, only 20 percent could be definitely classified as having this form of childhood background, whereas 52 percent showed no such possibilities. In addition, siblings of the transsexual, both older and younger, are normal and have not been affected by this familial background.

While the familial contribution to this syndrome does not seem to be supported by strong evidence—Pauly writes, for example, that the "intrafamily dynamics are varied and there is no common pattern which allows for generalization"—the distortion in sex identity commonly has occurred by the age of 3. Rejection in boys of the male role, ranging from simple rejection of masculine activities to the assumption of a female role and dress, does result in their being rejected by their peers. Transsexual patients are often socially withdrawn and friendless. Puberty increases their anxiety because the development of the secondary sex characteristics of the despised sex makes denial and fantasy even more difficult. Although male transsexuals have been known to marry and father children, they tend to have low levels of sexual activity unless they take up overt homosexual behaviors or can secure a change of sex through medical-surgical sex-conversion procedures.

Psychological therapy with these patients seems to enlighten the psycho-therapist but not the patient. No form of psychotherapy has proved to be helpful (Benjamin, 1966). Pauly has written (1965) that "intensive psychotherapy, hypnosis, aversive deconditioning, chemotherapy, and behavior therapy have been generally unsuccessful." On the other hand, the sex-conversion operation generally leaves the patient happy. Hastings reported a good social and emotional adjustment; Pauly reported that only 12 per cent of his cases were unsatisfactory; Benjamin found only 2 per cent unsatisfactory. This is a remarkable record of success for the most drastic kind of surgery and identity revision, on patients with histories of social withdrawal, alienation from peers and family, and a general culture-wide revulsion towards their abnormality.

It is interesting to speculate about the origin of this pathology. The literature seems clear in asserting that the normal causes for pathology, especially those from the family constellation, or from deviations in the mature body, seem absent. In 1961 Hampson and Hampson listed seven variables of sex: chromosomal, gonadal, hormonal, internal accessory reproductive structures, external genital morphology, sex of assignment and rearing, and gender identity (psychological sex). When they studied 110 pseudo and true hermaphrodites they found that the most critical factor seemed to be the assigned sex of rearing. But when they discuss the transsexual they state that "neither the purely genetic explanation nor the purely environmental explanation supplies all the answers to the questions posed by the disorders of psychologic sex (the transsexual)." They postulate that imprinting and critical periods could account for this phenomenon since these patients can recall having fantasies of being of the opposite sex as early as the age of 3 (Hampson and Hampson, 1961; Money, Hampson, and Hampson, 1957).

Stoller (1964) feels that gender identity is determined by the external genitalia, which includes the ascription of sex at birth and the consequent rearing, parental preference for a child of one sex or the other, and, finally, a "biological force." The term "biological force" is a name for the unknown factor inside of the mother, the fetus, or the infant which causes a child to later perceive himself as a member of the opposite sex despite his anatomical sex, his upbringing, and his parents' desires. It must be underscored that the patient's conviction that he is in the wrong body and can achieve happiness only by a change to the body of the opposite sex is in opposition to every force that the culture can pressure him with. This pathology, in the legal, psychological, and interpersonal sense, can bring him only rejection and grief.

What might Stoller's "biological force" be? What could be the origin of the "critical stage" described by the Hampsons? You will remember that the studies of the effect of testosterone upon animals revealed changes in the central nervous system, in the establishment of the masculinity and femininity of the organism independent of the reproductive organs. At birth the infant's genitals are large and well developed, but the central nervous system is not yet complete; that is, the developmental rates are different for the genital system and for the neural system. In that case it seems likely that the critical stages in development are also different. Organisms could reach normal *genital* development of one sex at the critical stage before the sex is established in the *neural* system's critical stage. If testosterone were present from outside sources during the critical neural-system stage of a female infant, the infant could have normal female genitals and a "masculine" brain. On the other hand, the male infant whose gonads produced insufficient testosterone at this second critical stage would be likely to have normal masculine genitals and a "female" brain. This could be the source of the feeling as he developed that he was trapped in the wrong body. If this situation were true we would find evidence, as Stoller suggests, of an early and irreversible core-gender identity "which is the result of a biological force sometimes powerful enough to contradict one's anatomy and upbringing."

It is interesting that most researchers report a ratio of between 3 and 4 to 1 (Hamburger, 1953; Pauly, 1965) and even 7 to 1 (Benjamin, 1966) in the proportion of male to female transsexual patients. I suspect that this may be a true finding and not simply the result of shyness on the part of female transsexuals. If our hypothesis is correct, the pathology will be more frequent in males. The female fetus is feminized by the sex hormones of the mother, and the animal data indicate that she would be female simply in the absence of testosterone—which, at least in the early stages of fetal development, her ovaries do not produce. The male fetus must produce and secrete testosterone from its own gonads in sufficient quantity and at the critical stage in order to produce masculinity or to offset the possible effect of circulating maternal hormones. This hypothesis suggests that masculinization of the central nervous system at the critical stage is more liable to error than feminization.

*The sexual identity of the human child and adult is not determined by his sex hormones or his reproductive system alone. The predispositions to sexual identity originating in biological forces are a part of a self-aware human being who more or less conforms to accepted cultural norms and who has internalized the cultural values into his individual psyche. No one of these factors will by itself determine identity; in a very real way they interact. But it is important to realize that sexual identity does have origins in early constitutional factors, and that experiential factors are not solely responsible for its development.*

## REFERENCES:

### Infant Differences

Bayley, Nancy 1964. Consistency of maternal and child behaviors in the Berkeley growth study. *Vita Humana* 7:73-95.

Bayley, Nancy, and E. S. Schaefer 1964. Correlations of maternal and child behaviors with the development of mental abilities. *Monographs of the Society for Research in Child Development* 29(6):97.

Bell, R. Q. 1960. Relations between behavior manifestations in the human neonate. *Child Development* 31:463-477.

Bell, R. Q., and Naomi S. Costello 1964. Three tests for sex differences in tactile sensitivity in the newborn. *Biologia Neonatorum*, pp. 335-347.

Bell, R. Q., and Joan F. Darling 1965. The prone head reaction in the human neonate: Relation with sex and tactile sensitivity. *Child Development* 36(4):943-949.

Escalona, Sibylle K., and Grace M. Heider 1959. *Prediction and outcome.* Basic Books, New York.

Garn, S. M. 1957. Roentgenogrammetric determinants of body composition. *Human Biology* 29:337-353.

Garn, S. M. 1958. Fat, body size and growth in the newborn. *Human Biology* 30:265-280.

Harlow, H. 1962. The heterosexual affectional response system in monkeys. *American Psychology* 17(1):1-9.

Jensen, G. D., and Ruth A. Bobbitt 1968. Monkeying with the mother myth. *Psychology Today* 1(12):41.

Kagan, J., and M. Lewis 1965. Studies of attention in the human infant. *Merrill-Palmer Quarterly* 11(2):95-127.

Kagan, J., and H. A. Moss 1962. From birth to maturity. Wiley, New York.

Knop, C. 1946. The dynamics of newly born babies. *Journal of Pediatrics* 29:721-728.

Lewis, M., J. Kagan, H. Campbell, and J. Kalafat 1965. The cardiac response as a correlate of attention in infants. Paper read at the American Psychological Association, Chicago.

Lewis, M., J. Kagan, and J. Kalafat 1965. Patterns of fixation in the young infant. Paper read at the Society for Research in Child Development, Minneapolis, Minn.

Lewis, M., J. Kagan, and J. Kalafat 1966. Patterns of fixation in the young infant. *Child Development* 37(2):331-341.

Lewis, M., W. Meyers, J. Kagan, and R. Grossberg 1963. Attention to visual patterns in infants. Paper presented at the Symposium on Studies of Attenion in Infants, American Psychological Association, August 1963, Philadelphia.

Lipsitt, L. P., and N. Levy 1959. Electrotactual threshold in the human neonate. *Child Development* 30:547-554.

Macfarlane, J. W., L. Allen, and M. P. Honzik 1954. *A developmental study of the behavior problems of normal children between twenty-one months and fourteen years.* University of California Press, Berkeley, Calif.

Murphy, Lois B., *et al.* 1962. *The widening world of childhood.* Basic Books, New York

Schaefer, E. S., and Nancy Bayley 1963. Maternal behavior, child behavior, and their intercorrelations from infancy through adolescence. *Monographs of the Society for Research in Child Development* 28(3).

Silverman, J. Attentional styles and the study of sex differences. In Mostofsky, D. (ed.), *Attention: contemporary studies and analysis.* Appleton, New York, in press.

Terman, L. M., and Leona E. Tyler 1954. Psychological sex differences. In Carmichael, L. (ed.), *A manual of child psychology.* 2nd ed. Wiley, New York, chap. 19.

**The Transsexual**

Benjamin, H. (ed.) 1966. *The transsexual phenomenon.* Julian Press, Inc., New York.

Green, R. 1966. Transsexualism: mythological, historical and cross-cultural aspects. In Banjamin, H. (ed.), *The transsexual phenomenon.* Julian Press, Inc., New York.

Hamburger, C. 1953. Desire for change of sex as shown by personal letters from 465 men and women. *Acta Endocrinologica* 14:361-375.

Hampson, J. S., and J. G. Hampson 1961. The otogenesis of sexual behavior in man. In Young, W. C. (ed.), *Sex and internal secretions,* vol. 2. Williams and Wilkins, Baltimore, Md., pp. 1401-1432.

Hastings, D. W., and J. A. Blum 1967. A transsexual research project at the University of Minnesota Medical School. *Lancet* 87(7).

Money, J., J. G. Hampson, and J. L. Hampson 1957. Imprinting and the establishment of gender role. *Archives of Neurology and Psychiatry* 77:333-336.

Pauly, L. 1965. Male psychosexual inversion: Transsexualism. *Archives of General Psychiatry* 13(2):172-181.

Stoller, R. J. 1967. Etiological factors in male transsexualism. *Transactions of the New York Academy of Science* 29(4):431-434.

Stoller, R. J. 1964. A contribution to the study of gender identity. *International Journal of Psychoanalysis* 45:220-226.

Stoller, R. J. 1965. Passing and the continuum of gender identity. In Marmor, J. (ed.), *Sexual inversion.* Basic Books, New York, pp. 190-210.

## SUGGESTED READINGS

Glen H. Elder, Jr., *Adolescent Socialization and Personality Development,* Chicago: Rand-McNally, 1968. Reviews current research on sex differences in later childhood, most of which is about males.

Eleanor Maccoby, (editor), *The Development of Sex Differences,* Stanford: Stanford University Press, 1966. One of the best collections of studies by psychologists, with an excellent annotated bibliography.

B. G. Rosenberg and Brian Sutton-Smith, *Sex and Identity,* New York: Holt, Rinehart, and Winston, 1972. Briefly and critiquely summarizes the major theoretical explanations for sex differences (ethological, biological, psychoanalytical, social learning, cultural, sociological).

# Sex and Politics

Lionel Tiger

Lionel Tiger was for a time roundly castigated by some feminists for arguing that there is a deep need for all-male bonds in society. Some saw this thesis to be an excuse for perpetuating the present system in which male groups in power exclude females. Close reading of Tiger does not entirely support this conclusion.

The notion of "male bond" implies that there are personal relationships important for the species in which males and females are not interchangeable. It means that males congregate in tightly knit groups with an intensity of feeling and intimacy similar to that found in parent-child or mating relationships. Tiger notes the existence of male bonds in some primates and traces their origins in the human species to biological needs of defense, food-gathering, and maintaining social order. He argues that these needs favored "genetic packages" which made males better hunters and females better child rearers, and, over time, also gave life to the secondary physical differences in men and women as we see them today. The social structure was affected in turn, with men predominating in politics and war.

Here Tiger examines in detail why politics has been to date a male territory, even in those countries where women have won the suffrage. The power of the male bonds makes the rapid expansion of women into politics seem unlikely. This presumes that Tiger's

---

arguments and interpretations of his data are the only plausible ones. Are they? And if the bond is in fact so effective in keeping women out of politics, does it follow that change is impossible?

---

At an anecdotal level, it is clear there is a close relationship between maleness, politics, and territory. The relationship may be causal, merely circumstantial, or the reflection of a syndrome. My own view is that it is the latter, and that when the syndrome is disrupted there are predictable consequences which we shall have occasion to consider later.

For the time being, let us see to what extent politics is a male enterprise and why this is so. Ardrey defines

> . . . the biological nation . . . [as] a social group containing at least two mature males which holds as an exclusive possession a continuous area of space, which isolates itself from others of its kind through outward antagonism, and which through joint defense of its social territory achieves leadership, co-operation, and a capacity for concerted action. It does not matter too much whether such a nation be composed of twenty-five individuals or two hundred and fifty million.[1]

From our point of view, the interesting feature of the definition is the specification that at least two mature males must form the core of the group; this is a similar conception to the spinal cord analogy ventured above. The evidence suggests it is valid to assert that political groups occupying territory are centered and dominated by hierarchies of adult—usually senior—males. (Age limits for officeholders, e.g. U.S. Presidents must be at least thirty-five, reflect general concern with the broad biological characteristics of age and the experience it may represent.) In his Introduction to *The Political Role of Women,* Maurice Duverger notes the hostility which exists in Europe to female political activity and alludes to the

> . . . traces of that primitive mentality which regards war as a "sport for men"; there is a similar tendency to regard politics as a man's affair. The club, the forum, debates, Parliament and political life in general are still considered to be typically masculine activities. . . . The existence of this more or less anti-feminist attitude, which despite an undeniable process of evolution, is still very strong, seems to be a directly observable fact so far as the recent survey is concerned.[2]

Duverger studied four countries intensively—France, the German Federal Republic, Norway, and Yugoslavia. He also gathered less detailed comparative data from fifteen other countries. The familiar but freshly striking general finding of his research is that women play a small role overall in the politics of their communities. Duverger explicitly denies that this is the result of biological differences: "There is nothing here to suggest an essential peculiarity in women's nature or a fundamental difference in men's and women's behavior."[3] This is a splendidly curious statement, in as much as it is the burden of Duverger's book to show that indeed there are differences in the political behavior of men and women. Presumably Duverger's implication is that those differences which do exist—and this argument is made at various points in his book—are chiefly the consequences of cultural tradition, economic opportunity, and conscious governmental decision.

Nonetheless it is with behavioral differences that we are concerned. These Duverger's evidence affirms. Of particular relevance to our concern with positions of generalized dominance and access to a public forum is that—invariably—there are fewer women in any organization the higher up its hierarchy a count is made:

> This progressive decline in women's influence as the higher levels of leadership are reached is not only noticeable in the structure of the State and political organs, but is also to be found in the government service, the political parties, the trade unions, private business, etc. Nor are there any perceptible signs of improvement in this respect. Although the difference in the proportions of men and women non-voters sometimes tends to lessen in certain countries, nothing similar can be noted at the Parliamentary and governmental levels. The percentage of women members of parliament, for instance, is hardly increasing. On the contrary, it tends to fall after the first elections in which women have had the suffrage, and to become stabilized at a very low level.[4]

For example, after female suffrage was introduced in Japan, thirty-five females were elected in national contests, but this has now dropped to eleven. American experience suggests females are less likely to vote for females than males for males.[5] Canadian material corroborates this.[6] In Australia, though females had the vote earlier than in the U.S. or the U.K. and did not have to struggle for it, the relative unimportance of voting is expressed in the fact that "over the entire period since women were eligible to sit in the Australian parliament, only a fraction of 1 percent have been women."[7]

Duverger notes an important disparity between women's voting behavior and their political behavior. There is considerable similarity in male and female *voting* behavior, but there is an extreme dissimilarity in male and female *political* behavior. Not only is there an extensive quantitative difference in political participation, there is also a qualitative one:

> In party leadership, in senior administrative posts, in parliaments and in governments, the few women included concentrate on specialized matters, such as health, education, motherhood, family welfare, housing, etc.—that is, on all problems which, in the general opinion, are considered to be of special interest to women . . . there are signs . . . of a very definite aggravation of this tendency toward specialization.[8]

While, as Duverger notes, it is not difficult to counter the various arguments which men raise to exclude females from politics, nonetheless

> the small influence of women in State leadership is in large measure due to women's own inertia. . . . Not only do women show little desire to win a place in political leadership, but the great majority of them accept the system of justification invented by men to rationalize their standing aside from it. Curiously, they sometimes seem to be more uncompromising than men in this regard, and more anti-feminist.[9]

Duverger provides some cross-cultural data on female participation which are worth summarizing in some detail. With the exception of the U.S.S.R., where 17 percent of the Surpreme Soviet (which has very little power) is female, 5 percent appears to be the maximum of female participation in various parliaments. It is a maximum "seldom attained": Netherlands, 5 to 6 percent; French Assembly, 3.6 percent; Norway, 4 percent; U.K., 3 percent; United States Congress, 2 percent.

> In the local and municipal bodies, the proportion is seldom higher and often lower. . . . At the governmental level, women play an even smaller part.[10]

> . . . in 1949, out of 59 countries where women had the right to vote, women held ministerial office in only 11; none of these countries was a leading power; no country had more than one woman minister; and Rumania was the only country where the ministerial office held by a woman was of any real political importance (foreign affairs). . . . Not only is an extremely small proportion of women admitted to association

> with the government, but the number does not appear to be increasing. On the contrary, in the countries where women's right to vote was recognized over 30 years ago, there is a decided tendency toward a stabilization of the number of women members of parliament—after an initial surge in the years immediately following the electoral reform.[11]

There is no evidence that these situations vary between societies with more and less liberal views on feminist principles and the political equality of the sexes. For example, the United States is commonly thought to be feminist and in general women are supposed to wield considerable influence. They are the most well-educated female population in history; they are economically advantaged. Yet the U.S. has one of the smallest proportions of female members in its national government—about 2 percent.

Of special interest is the fact that, in communities in which female representation has increased, this has been the result of the effort of left-wing parties:

> . . . it is the left-wing parties, particularly the Socialist and Communist parties, which have done most to increase the number of women entering Parliament or holding office in the government—an attitude which may well appear paradoxical, since women electors . . . are, in the majority, conservative. One might almost say that parties which do the most for women are the parties for which women do the least.[12]

For example, the French Communist party has elected the greatest number of females to office. Yet it commands the smallest proportion of women voters of any major party. In view of the traditional theory of democratic politics, which contains the proposition that political parties broadly represent the groups electing them, this is indeed paradoxical, and of considerable relevance to the notion of representative democracy. There is another distortion of the theory of representative democracy; this reflects the fact that only exceptionally have women's suffragette organizations actually succeeded in securing female suffrage: "This extension of the suffrage seems attributable to the two world wars rather than to the work of women's associations."[13] Even before this time, for example in America, female suffrage occurred first in states where there was no strong female agitation for the vote, but where females' votes were desired by men for their own particular political purposes.[14]

The changes in women's rights were effected largely by men. It could not be otherwise because usually—as in Switzerland, for example—men must vote on the very constitutional amendments accepting female suffrage. Significantly, in many countries women received the right to vote as the result of executive decrees by revolutionary provisional governments which later ratified such decrees in the new terms of their drastically won legitimacy.

This suggests the depth and complexity of the connection between political order and male dominance. It will be discussed more fully below. In one description of the constellation of attitudes and actions in this area, Young and Bacdayan demonstrate a provocative if bizarre correlation between menstrual taboos, the position of women in communities, and the extent to which communities are politically, religiously, and socially rigid.[15] They sketch the kind of variation which may occur in this area and show how the notion of "woman" a community holds—of which attitudes to menstruation are an important index—occurs not capriciously but as a function of political system.

Thus where women have been allowed the vote—and it is essential to bear in mind that even voting is, in terms of an individual's participation in the polity, a relatively unimportant action—this has apparently been largely the result of effort by males on females' behalf. Not infrequently it has been associated with reformist or revolutionary changes in political structure. . . .

The data indicate that the attitudes of males and females to female participation in the political arena remain stable. Apparently even major changes in political form and ideology can have little effect on the role of women. For example, during the Nazi era in Germany, the female role was—in the famous phrase—supposed to revolve around *"Kinder, kirche, und küchen."* Goebbels elaborated the position:

> . . . the National Socialist Movement is in its nature a masculine movement. . . . While man must give to life the great lines and forms, it is the task of woman out of her inner fullness and inner eagerness to fill these lines and forms with color. The realms of directing and shaping . . . politics . . . must without qualification be claimed by man. When we eliminate women from public life, it is not because we want to dispense with them but rather because we want to give them back their essential honor. . . . The outstanding and highest calling of woman is always that of wife and mother and it would be an unthinkable misfortune if we allowed ourselves to be turned from this point of view.[16]

Until Hitler specifically organized women's groups—defined as such—the female Nazi party membership was less than 3 percent. German women never undertook military service, even in the Second World War. Now, after the war, an at least superficially quite different political structure exists. But females are still excluded from or do not participate in party political leadership, and it appears that little substantial difference exists between current attitudes of the community to female political activity and those in evidence before the trauma of the war and its effects.

It has already been noted that females in the U.S. have not so far successfully penetrated higher political circles in numbers in any sense related to the potential political influence which could be based on their 51 percent voting strength. Tiny numbers occupy high posts in the judicial and administrative hierarchies; "under the past 3 administrations women have comprised a constant percent–2.4–of a rising number: 79 of 3,273 in 1951-52; 84 of 3,491 in 1958-59; 93 of 3,807 in 1961-62."[17] Changes of political administration appear to mark no effective changes in appointments of females to the Federal Administrative Service, though it is thought that conditions are becoming more favorable to the employment of women in high posts. This is because of decreasing resistance by men (though few political inner circles are free of it) and because females may in the future prepare themselves more self-consciously for careers–which may include politics–and may be psychologically and experientially better equipped to compete for high office.

But the significant point remains that the political elites of the U.S. and other societies are male. The backroom boys of legend do exist. They have not yet accepted women either easily or in any numbers. In a study of the American elite,[18] C. Wright Mills makes no reference to females, while in his outstanding analysis of stratification patterns in Canada, John Porter does not find it necessary to be directly concerned with females.[19] Lipset's elaborate study offers no contrary evidence.[20]

The exclusion of females is not a phenomenon peculiar to the wealthier Euro-American societies. The error is commonly made that matriarchal societies are societies where females dominate social and political affairs. But the truth is that matriarchy is a principle of hereditary succession, not a political pattern, and should in usage properly be replaced by matrilineality. In his study of "primitive" society, Lowie flatly states that matrilineal descent patterns do not symptomize female government. There are a very few instances,

> . . .they can be counted on the fingers of one hand, . . . in which women either exercise unusual property rights or play

> a remarkable part in public life. . . . Even among the Iroquois (where women play a role in the election of chiefs) no woman had a place in the supreme council of the league. . . . A genuine matriarchate is nowhere to be found.[21]

Allen's comprehensive study of Melanesian secret and age-grade societies reveals that the vast majority of these are male societies. There are "no true examples in Melanesia of bisexual associations—those in which females may have some role confine females to less than full membership."[22] Without indicating what the reasons for the probability are, Allen states:

> In all probability there are a considerable number of unrecorded women's associations entered by rites of initiation. The only definite examples that I know of are the women's secret societies of the Seniang and Lambumbi districts of Malekula Island in the northern New Hebrides.[23]

Allen's major reason for the statement of probability (personal communication) is that the majority of field-workers are males and would be less likely to discover female groups than male groups, and less likely to be told about them, given the severe intersexual hostility which characterizes many communities of Melanesia. His argument is echoed by Paulme, who suggests that social science is male-centric, if only because the majority of its practitioners are males who are disinclined and possibly incapable of perceiving a view of female behavior substantially different from the conventional "Western" one.[24] Another argument that social science is male-centric is put by Betty Friedan.[25] Friedan is particularly anxious to demonstrate the sexually biased nature of Freudian theory (see her Chapter Five), and illustrates the important consequences which potentially follow a theory based on inadequate data and interpreted without objectivity about female socio-sexual behavior. An additional impediment—and perhaps a more consequential one—to the use of Freudian theory to explain behavior is that the theory has been so influential as to constitute a feature of the very cultures it seeks to explain. Precisely in those societies in which Freudian and neo-Freudian analysts are numerically and intellectually powerful—for example, in the U.S.A.—lay folklore as well as professional theory is structured around the expectation that the behavior Freud identified will appear. (While this is in one sense a tribute to the credibility and possible correctness of Freudian theory, it also constitutes a barrier to its disconfirmability. This does not mean Freudian hypotheses should not be used, but only with special care and consciousness.)

Given the argument I have been making, one would predict that there will be far fewer female organizations than male ones. Where they do exist, the relative obscurity of the female organizations and their apparent unimportance for the macro-life of the community is striking and provocative. I am not saying females do not aggregate (in Melanesia and elsewhere) for some purposes, such as childcare, gathering, and farming, or for simple gregariousness. But those female organizations which do exist bear much less direct relationship than do men's organizations to the political structure of their communities and the establishment of the dominance hierarchy. Nor do they appear to be as persistent over time. Even where female organizations are relatively well established such as among the Mende of Sierra Leone, it is the male *Poro* secret society which "In the political field . . . exercises an overriding influence which is both direct and indirect and only *Poro* members can have political office in the chiefdom."[26] The *Sande*, which deals with women's affairs, and the *Humoi,* which is concerned with the sexual conduct of the community, do not formally impinge upon the political process in Mende society. The head of the Humoi society—a woman—may attend meetings of *Poro* high officials, but she is not permitted to participate. Significantly, even her role is symbolically restricted, because she is assumed to be invisible during meetings to all members except the Grand Tasso.[27]

Interestingly, one common way in which females acquire high office is by being close and politically active relatives of senior politicians who die. This is perhaps the most obvious and certainly the easiest way in which women have come to occupy high posts. Various cases come to mind: Mrs. S. R. D. Bandaranaike of Ceylon, Madame Ghandi (daughter of Nehru), Mrs. Maurine Neuberger, Eleanor Roosevelt, Jennie Lee (wife of Aneurin Bevan), Madame Sun Yat-sen, Lady Gaitskill, Lady Nancy Astor, Lady Iveagh, Lena Jeger. "A curious fact of political life in Canada is that if a widow stands for her late husband's seat in a federal by-election she is almost sure to win."[28] The explanation for this is commonsensical. But at another level the matter may be rather more complex. Undoubtedly part of the reason for the appointment of widows to high office is the sense of gratitude which the deceased politician's colleagues may feel for his efforts during his lifetime. Internal party equilibrium may be maintained by honoring the memory of an individual whose supporters remain important and ambitious. There is probably an element of "pensioning off" a widow whose husband's death might have left her financially deprived unless a post was arranged for her. More simply, the widow's experience during her husband's career and her contacts with his professional colleagues might draw attention to her possible talents in the political field.

But a more interesting if more fugitive process may be at work when either professional politicians or electors or both give political posts to female relatives of deceased dominant males. In many vertebrate communities females assume the status of their male mates; in primates the phenomenon is sufficiently closely related to small-scale human class structures for one ethologist to propose that comparable mechanisms operate in primates as well as humans.[29] For example, in Hutterite communities in Alberta, the post of Chief Cook—the highest female post—is normally filled by the wife of either the Preacher or the Boss, the two highest ranking males.[30] A Maratha princess of India traditionally had the responsibility of leading "her troops in person when there was no husband or son to do so."[31]

Perhaps females possess the "releaser" which stimulates people to follow them mainly when they embody or share the "charisma" or dominance of a closely related male. Otherwise they neither inspire the confidence nor channel the energies of potential supporters—or so the facts of the matter starkly suggest.

Thus, that females only rarely dominate authority structures may reflect females' underlying inability—at the ethological level of "pattern-releasing" behavior—to affect the behavior of subordinates. However, this general handicap apparently can be overcome by those females who have obviously participated in the use of power through their closely related men. More than any other factor, this appears to lend efficaciousness to females' otherwise ineffective political efforts. Of course, this is similar to the general process of transmission of charisma from one person to another which occurs in the development of dynastic political traditions. A retired incumbent's endorsement of an aspiring candidate is part of the same process of transmission. Female succession is only one factor in the complex process of maintaining social order. But it may be of vital significance to the understanding of this process to recognize that the division of labor along sexual lines predictably occurs in any community and that the dominant political roles in this division are disproportionately assigned to males.

Of course, many of the reasons for female non-participation in higher politics arise out of a variety of straightforward social situations, such as the complexities of the role of child-rearing, the legal propertylessness of females in some communities which must inhibit their freedom of political action, the fact that often they may not easily enter professions such as law which may be a typical prelude to political careers, and the simple fact that females are generally less well educated and have fewer broad opportunities for political experience than males (though women with grown children may have more available time).

But I have been stressing that there are other underlying species-regularities involved. First, that women leaders do not inspire "followership" chiefly because they are women and not only because of the consequences of those factors noted above; secondly, even if they want to, women cannot become political leaders because males are strongly predisposed to form and maintain all-male groups, particularly when matters of moment for the community are involved. The suggestion is that a combination of these two factors has been the basis for the hostility and difficulty those females have faced who have aspired to political leadership. This has been the basis of the tradition of female non-involvement in high politics, and not the tradition itself. Cultural forms originally express the underlying "genetically programed behavioral propensities." In their turn, such cultural forms maintain—as tradition—an enduring solution to the recurrent problem of assigning leadership and followership roles. In this connection, Margaret Mead writes about "zoomorphizing Man": "Culture in the sense of man's species-characteristic method of meeting problems of maintenance, transformation, and transcendence of the past is an abstraction from our observations on particular cultures."[32] This is then another way of looking at how broad political patterns may predictably emerge from the more detailed and programed patterns of different behavior of males and females.

Some females may indeed penetrate some high councils. They become ministers of governments, ambassadors, and so on. A few may receive assignments which are not "feminine" in their implication, such as Golda Meir, the Israeli Prime Minister, and Barbara Castle, U.K. Secretary of Productivity and Employment. It is important to know what happens to the "backroom boys" under such circumstances. Do they retire to an even more secluded chamber? Does the lady become "one of the boys?"

Formal conduct of business is one thing. Constitutional and other legal constraints may permit successfully dominant females an effective role. But no one can control informal activity. Card-playing, hunting, fishing, all-male clubs, and so on may provide that further back room in which the outlines of policy and the distribution of power are determined. How pertinent are, for example, the hunting and fishing facilities which wealthy companies in the U.S.A., the U.K., Germany, etc., maintain for the entertainment of business colleagues? Paradoxically, the attention paid by many corporations to the wives of promotable executives underlies the dependency of females on the male hierarchy and their need to be committed to advance company purposes and not their own. Corporation wives—like wives of men in many spheres of activity—must be willing to subserve their own interests to their husbands' and their husbands' employers. They must also be willing to withdraw from conversations or events involving "the man" or "the Company." Clearly this is an effect of social pressures and conventions; it does not occur unambiguously in all groups, and in some—certain sectors of academe for example—women are less likely to be thus subservient to the male group. It is also clear that this pattern is as much a function of power as of maleness, and it can be argued that powerful *people* are being deferred to, who happen to be male.

On the other hand, the contention here is that this association is no accident. There is an extreme case which could throw light on the whole situation. Presently, in the formal sphere, one female or several can become members of powerful bodies. What would happen to these groups and their power should females come to predominate in them? In a cabinet of fifteen persons, one, two, or even four females might be acceptable to the remaining males and the voters. But were there nine or ten? Significantly, even in the Soviet Union, which has elected as many as 17 percent of females to the Duma, the Supreme Council—which has the effective power—has occasionally contained one female, but more often none. Were a cabinet to become dominated by females, probably its role would be circumscribed. We can predict that other—male—power centers would emerge to withdraw crucial powers from the female-dominated body.

Perhaps we can draw an analogy with the racial encounters in the U.S.A., and with what happens when blacks move into white residential areas. What is virtually an all-white area becomes a predominantly black one. This is not because property values decline (often they increase), but because of some apparent caste-like response by whites who prefer not to live in close proximity to blacks. Undoubtedly there will be a number of social and economic changes in any neighborhood when a new social group moves in. But the chief underlying reason for the exit of the whites appears to center about status factors. George DeVos has made a cogent analysis of two kinds of exploitation of social groups by social groups: instrumental and expressive. The former is well understood—it involves money, jobs, consumer goods, etc. As DeVos makes clear, the latter is well analyzed:[33]

> . . . expressive exploitations are related directly to the irrational and unconscious psychological processes and motives characteristic of man's complex mental structure. The motives behind such exploitation are less readily perceived than those leading to instrumental exploitation. . . . Expressive exploitation, although universal in one form or other, is most visibly institutionalized in societies that are rigidly segregated by birth or occupational groupings. Inherent is a biological and/or religious concept of unalterable inferiority which distinguishes one group of men from another. In external group or cultural relationships this patterning of belief is apparent in the justification of wars. Within a society, it justifies maintaining a fixed social order of dominance and subordination from birth to death.

DeVos sees the expressive exploitation of females as a marked feature of only some societies; in its less marked forms it occurs in most if not all communities. The racial or caste analogy may be instructive here. When white people live among blacks they are held to acquire characteristics of the low-status "impurity" which the prejudiced community at large attributes to blacks. In the same way, when males work in occupational groups in which there are many females, such as interior decoration, hairdressing, acting, or ballet, it is frequently assumed or alleged that they are effeminate.

The questions can be posed: Does a similar process occur when groups wielding power become predominated by females? Is female power low-status power? If so, can a community accept dominance of its powerful bodies by females? Based on the data and extrapolation from the results of experimental and accidental attempts to alter the sexual balance of power, the answer is a secure if tentative "No, the male-centered dominant group recurs." To recall my original analogy: it may be a species-characteristic of *Homo sapiens* that the "spinal column" of *Homo sapiens'* community must be very predominantly male. And to return briefly to black-white relations in America, the interesting argument has been raised that the effectiveness and significance of black protest politics is related to "the masculinization" of black politics. Namely, to the efforts of comparatively young black males to establish patterns of community organization and political action which supersede those possible in "traditional" black American society—a post-slavery society in which disenfranchised and economically marginal males could create no communal political "spinal cord" and in which females were inevitably the effective social and economic people around growing children. This has had numerous well-reported effects on black family life; the masculinization of black corporate life remains a relatively unresearched but crucial subject.

The upshot of all this is the contention that: male dominance coupled with sexual dimorphism occurs cross-culturally; it may be a phenomenon rooted in the nature of *Homo sapiens.* Accepting the first half of the statement does not require accepting the second. Simply, a view of the close links between politics and socio-sexual role may provide a picture of political activity with a useful emphasis on the factor of maleness in determining the participants in and forms of politics. Harold Lasswell briefly notes that "Political life seems to sublimate many homosexual trends. Politicians characteristically work together in little cliques and clubs, and many of them show marked difficulties in reaching a stable heterosexual adjustment." He also indicates that homosexual activity in the military is an important factor requiring analysis.[34]

Lasswell probably overestimates the importance of the purely erotic aspects of homo- and heterosexuality and underestimates the social-organizational aspects. If it is true as I have been proposing that human males characteristically form all-male groups which tend to have political or quasi-political functions, and that they seek to exclude females from these groups, then this is one explanation for the male near-monopoly of high political office. It supplements the explanation which is based upon the possibility that male political dominance is a reflection both of human evolution and contemporary traditions and socio-economic constants. The implication of this for the study of politics is that it becomes possible—indeed necessary—to regard political groups which are unisexual as possessing sexual (non-erotic) bases.

In trying to find out about the Nazis in Hitler's party, for example, in addition to asking the questions: What kind of people were they, and how did they live with others? another question is necessary too, since it promotes the collection of particularly pertinent data: What kind of *men* were they, how did they express their maleness, how did they interact with other men? Had they particular insecurities as *men* which drove them to identify so eventfully with Hitler and his theory? Why did Hitler marry Eva Braun just before his suicide? What happened in that very special male bond of senior Nazis? Again, I must stress that I do not imply that the foregoing comments invalidate the studies of politics which have been made and are being made. What is suggested is that an additional dimension of understanding may follow an appreciation of the special nature of unisexual political interaction. A study such as Eisenstadt's,[35] which is constructed with great skill on the basis of immense erudition, could be augmented by an assessment of the importance of sexuality in creating and constraining such diverse groups as William Whyte's Boston "Corner Boys" and the Nyakusa age-villagers. On the basis of the argument about bonding and evolution, perhaps it is clearer why I think the sex of politicians is extremely important, why the most dominant politicians are usually male, why the introduction of formal female political equality has not had more obvious structural and behavioral effects, and why an ethological view of the sexually based group dynamics of political interaction is useful for the cross-cultural understanding of political behavior.

These are issues which are still justifiably controversial. Perhaps a brief personal note is relevant here, simply to indicate that the scientific argument I have been making and the data I have presented appear to lead to very different conclusions about the ease of extending female political influence than—as a citizen—I am predisposed to seek. In other words, my political bias is toward a rapid and meaningful expansion of women's participation in and effect on politics. But my sociological work suggests the difficulty of achieving this because more than just routine education and emancipation may be involved. Perhaps rather major and truly radical restructuring of political society will be necessary before what may be a deep predisposition can be overcome in the name of equity. This is not to beg the question about the "desirability" of achieving this equity. Nor is it any guarantee that my conclusions are correct, because my personal political beliefs and my scientific conclusions do not coincide. But perhaps it is of interest to some readers to be informed directly about this (finally methodological) matter of what a social scientist brings personally to an investigation, particularly since my statement of the results of this study has stimulated some commentators to accuse me—unfairly, I must protest—of being a male chauvinist.

## FOOTNOTES AND REFERENCES

1. Robert Ardrey, *The Territorial Imperative,* Atheneum Press, New York, 1966, p. 191.

2. Maurice Duverger, *The Political Role of Women,* UNESCO, Paris, 1955, p. 10.

3. ibid., p. 122.

4. ibid., p. 123.

5. Nona B. Brown, "Inquiry into the Feminine Mind," *New York Times Magazine* (12 April 1964).

6. Kathy Hassard, "Spriit of Feminism Political Lack Today," *Vancouver Sun* (2 October 1963). Even in the relatively "modern izing" government of Pierre Elliot Trudeau, there is only one woman out of 264 members of the House of Commons.

7. Thelma Hunt, "Australian Women," *The Australian Quarterly,* 35, 1 (March 1963), p. 80.

8. Duverger, op. cit., p. 124.

9. ibid., p. 126.

10. ibid., p. 145.

11. ibid., p. 146.

12. ibid., p. 147.

13. Duverger, op. cit., p. 139.

14. In the nineteenth century, the only states with female suffrage were Wyoming, Utah, Colorado, and Idaho. For an excellent account of these early and subsequent changes in American female political activity, see Alan P. Grimes, *The Puritan Ethic and Woman Suffrage,* Oxford University Press, New York, 1967. See also Andrew Sinclair, *The Emancipation of the American Woman,* Harper and Row, New York, 1966.

15. Frank W. Young and Albert A. Bacdayan, "Menstrual Taboos and Social Rigidity," *Ethnology,* 4, 2 (April 1965).

16. Goebbels, then Minister of Propaganda, quoted in Clifford Kirkpatrick, *Nazi Germany: Its Women and Family Life,* Bobbs-Merrill, New York, 1938, p. 116.

17. Margaret Mead and Frances B. Kaplan (eds.), *American Women,* Charles Scribner's and Sons, New York, 1965, pp. 72 and 74.

18. C. Wright Mills, "The Structure of Power in American Society," *British Journal of Sociology,* 60, 1 (March 1958). See also Mills's *The Power Elite,* Oxford University Press, 1956.

19. John Porter, *The Vertical Mosaic,* University of Toronto Press, 1965.

20. Lipset, *Political Man,* Doubleday, New York, 1966.

21. Robert Lowie, *Primitive Society,* Liveright, New York, 1947.

22. Allen, *Rites de Passage,* Melbourne University Press (in press).

23. ibid.

24. See Denise Paulme (ed.), *Women of Tropical Africa,* University of California Press, 1964, p. 1.

25. Betty Friedan, *The Feminine Mystique,* W. W. Norton, New York, 1963.

26. Kenneth L. Little, "The Role of the Secret Society in Cultural Specialization," *American Anthropologist,* 51, 1 (March 1949), pp. 204-5.

27. F. W. Butt-Thompson, *West African Secret Societies,* Witherby, London, 1929, p. 72.

28. Jean Sharp, "Widows Are Often Successful Running for Political Office," *Montreal Star* (22 December 1964).

29. William R. S. Russell, personal communication.

30. Vernon Serl, personal communication.

31. A. S. Attekar, *The Position of Women in Hindu Civilization,* Motilal Banarsidas, Benares, 1956, p. 22.

32. Mead, *Continuities in Cultural Evolution,* Yale University Press. New Haven, 1964.

33. George DeVos, "Conflict, Dominance and Exploitation in Human Systems of Social Segregation: Some Theoretical Perspectives from the Study of Personality in Culture," in Anthony de Reuck and Julie Knight (eds.), op. cit. See also Chapters One to Three of Andrew Sinclair, op. cit., for discussion of the racial analogy.

34. Harold Lasswell, *Psychopathology and Politics,* Viking Press, New York, 1960, p. 178.

35. Eisenstadt, *From Generation to Generation,* Free Press, New York, 1955.

## SUGGESTED READINGS

Kirsten Amundsen, *The Silenced Majority,* Englewood Cliffs, N.J.: Prentice-Hall, 1971. Documents the exclusion of American women from political and economic power.

G. William Domhoff, *Who Rules America?* Englewood Cliffs, N.J.: Prentice-Hall, 1967. One of many recent studies arguing that a small elite of males have most of the formal power in America.

Robert D. Hess and Judith V. Torney, *The Development of Political Attitudes in Children,* Chicago: Aldine, 1967. Shows how young girls and boys display very different attitudes toward political concepts and activities.

Lionel Tiger and Robin Fox, *The Imperial Animal,* New York: Holt, Rinehart, and Winston, 1971. The most recent development in their ideas about sex and politics, also highly readable and provocative.

# The Feminized Male

**Patricia Cayo Sexton**

Patricia Sexton's discussion of boys in schools substantiates Bardwick's thesis that men in our society are prevented from being "masculine," which means aggressive, autonomous, masterly, adventurous, tough, and technologically skillful. Instead they are being "feminized" because it is women who set the standards of adult behavior in the home and in school—the two areas in which society traditionally permits them to dominate the power structure. Sexton disapproves of this trend, yet at the same time argues that women should receive the same education and have the same opportunities as men. Her position seems equivocal: she longs for truly masculine men yet advocates equality for women. Can we have both?

Sexton's thesis is a good example of a scholarly work that builds on assumptions that have never been subjected to scientific verification. Nowhere in her book does Sexton explain why she accepts and restates the traditional notions of masculinity and femininity. Do you find it surprising that two female scholars (Bardwick and Sexton) would develop similar theories, i.e., that men are the ones who suffer because their "masculinity" is being repressed?

Whether or not one accepts her position, Sexton challenges one of the arguments set forth by those who want to see all sexism eliminated; namely, must all sex role differences go? (Winick's

---

paper later in this volume argues that they need not.) Furthermore, how do we know that we are producing more "masculinized females" than in the past? Couldn't this concern have its roots in the fear shared by many, of giving women more power and control in society? And to what extent might these fears be related to insecurities about sexuality? How could you get data to answer these questions?

---

## L'ACADEMIE FEMININE

In public elementary schools, 85 percent of all teachers are women. In all public schools, women are 68 percent of the total. Men are now a bare majority in secondary schools. On the other hand, in higher education, women are a small minority of teaching faculties—and are heavily concentrated in the arts, education, nursing, social work, English, languages, and the social sciences.

Women multiply in the school when men are engaged elsewhere, during times of prosperity or war. During World War I, women were 86 percent of all public school teachers, and during World War II the figure was only slightly lower.

Though run at the top by men, schools are essentially feminine institutions, from nursery through graduate school. In the school, women set the standards for adult behavior, and many favor students, male and female, who most conform to their own behavior norms—polite, clean, obedient, neat and nice ones. While there is nothing wrong with the code, for those who like it, it does not give boys (or girls either) much room to flex their muscles—physical or intellectual.

Putting a man, any man, in place of women in school will not do. A man who is less than a man can be more damaging to boys than a domineering mother. The chances of getting feminized men in the school are fairly good because those eligible and willing, given present hiring codes and salaries, are usually those who made it through a feminine school system without conflict or failure.

One is inclined to say that the younger the student, the more feminine the tone of the school seems to be. But, then, some graduate programs seem far more oppressive to the male temperament than do kindergartens, even though there are more female teachers present in the latter. What does seem clear is that the system is spun round, like a cocoon, with threads woven by women and feminized males. The signs are found everywhere, in curriculum, standards, values, systems of reward, methods of instruction, personnel, remoteness from power and reality, and dispersal of authority.

To mention authority is not to suggest that the school is either too permissive or too authoritarian, too easy or too punishing, too chaotic or too disciplined. It is a difficult point, but the sketchy evidence we have about the way organizations operate indicates that they can be either very strict or very loose and still permit optimal masculine growth, depending on how authority is used, by whom, and to what ends. For example, the military is certainly not the least masculine of institutions, yet it is run with firm authority. The Wild West was an era of perhaps excessive masculinity, yet it ran almost without law and order. One would assume, based partly on speculation and some psychological evidence, that freedom and consent nourish the masculine temperament and are as essential to natural sex growth as protein is to body growth. But man does not live on protein and license alone. These must be taken along with other fuels.

The signs of femininity are even found in the sounds people make, quite apart from the words they speak. Many academicized people have a certain identifying sound—feminine and vaguely reptilian—which is made often by them, but rarely by others. The characterizing sound of the schoolmarm is *shhh* and among the university elites (faculty and students) the corresponding sound is *hisss*. Both are meant, like the serpent's rattler, to express hostile intent, and both often succeed in suppressing the expression of others. Made from behind closed lips, the sound does not always identify its source. Its expression is no act of brave personal dissent, but instead permits anonymity from antagonists. It is a cat sound—feline, sibilant, "female."

The schools mainly teach the words and number symbols of reading, writing, arithmetic. One hardly ever sees the *things* these symbols stand for. Deeds and actions are rarely the substance of school instruction, activity being viewed as disruptive of academic study. Schools set the standards—followed too religiously by others who judge people—by which people are measured. They are the academic measures of ability to deal with symbols on paper, rather than measures of performance or creativity.

School words tend to be the words of women. They have their own sound and smell, perfumed or antiseptic. Just as there are dialects of class, occupation, and region, so there are distinguishable dialects of gender. Women use different words, stress them differently, put them together in special ways, use them for different purposes, write them differently—and usually much more legibly. Boys, for example, usually prefer tough and colorful short words—while teachers and girls lean toward longer, more floral and opaque synonyms. School words are clean and refined—sugar and spice, and other things nice—idealized and as remote from physical things as the typical schoolmarm from the tough realities of ordinary life.

*Active* word usage, as in *speaking,* is usually discouraged in school; students are expected to speak only when addressed. Talking—a far more aggressive act than reading, listening, or even writing—is a favorite mode of male verbal activity. Even boys who refuse to read or write usually like to talk, but on their own terms. It is the school's most troublesome job to suppress most forms of spontaneous oral expression, and to keep boys quiet and in their seats.

The classroom cannot, of course, be an oral free-for-all. Nor can our primers become indistinguishable from locker room talk. But some of the guts of male talk should be left intact. A boy would probably be run out of school for imitating Norman Mailer's prose, yet Mailer is one of our most gifted writers. Many well-meaning efforts to add the vernacular to our formal language look silly and seem artificially pasted on top of old packages. Still, the school primers need not fall so far behind the times. Much of the vernacular gets into formal language anyhow, enriching and simplifying it. More is needed, especially from the style, if not the vocabulary, of male talk. Some males are able to blend action words from the street with those that pass for proper English. Let them be the teachers of words and written language. And let there be more time in school for boys to talk and say what they want to each other.

Some science is taught in schools, but usually as words which are detached from things, from doing and discovering. Thus, the magic and adventure of science are missing. Physics, an academic subject with some natural appeal to average boys, is offered only to honor students, and often only in an unpalatable form, loaded with memorization and excessive detail, and drained of the spirit of scientific inquiry. So it is that many boys (and girls) with a natural interest in what lies at the heart of physical reality are bypassed. As for technology, aside from shop classes, which at least offer slow or troubled boys a chance to move around, there is a great glaring void, filled in by long hours of paper work.

Methods of school instruction require little more than passive receiving and repeating. The student listens to the teacher. He reads the book. He memorizes and repeats what the book and teacher have said. His "learning" is passive and feminine, not active. He sits, listens, reads, writes, repeats, and speaks when spoken to. Thus learning is reduced to a body of facts to be noted and stored, rather than a method of active and rigorous inquiry and a way to examine and master one's environment.

The feminized school simply bores many boys; but it pulls some in one of two opposite directions. If the boy absorbs school values, he may become feminized himself. If he resists, he is pushed toward school failure and rebellion. Increasingly, boys are drawn to female norms. The attraction is the rainbow that lies at the end of graduation with honor, the school diploma, the college degree. More than ever before in human history, a boy's fate will be determined by the number of diplomas he gets and where he gets them. As long as society and employers generally regard diplomas as *the* badge of merit, boys will be pulled ever deeper into a system that rewards conformity to feminine standards. While the rainbow lies ahead, voices at the rear (friends, or even parents, if they want a real boy) urge him to be himself and become an autonomous person. Following this course means trouble in school, but being your own man can, for many boys, be worth the sacrifice of gold stars in class.

Of course, school achievement is not identical with life achievement, though the two are very closely related. Many exceptional boys, of course, can break all school rules and still rise to the top in life. Nor are those who head the most powerful organizations usually the most feminized males. More often they are those who have managed, through fate or some ploy, to escape the feminizing influence of school and society. Many boys know better than female teachers that academic learning has little to do with what goes on in the real world, that it does not always produce top results in real life.

Elites in America, unlike the British (who tend to be born to privilege), have at least avoided the *extremes* of feminization. Our corporate and government elites have not come exclusively from school honor rolls—or from among those who went to the "right" schools and come from the "right" families. Though we may deplore the lack of vigor and humanity at the top, relative to elites in other societies we may be further ahead than we think.

Many top American political and corporate leaders have been poor or average scholars in college (Dwight Eisenhower, Franklin D. Roosevelt, Lyndon Johnson, Nelson Rockefeller, etc.), and we have not followed the Latin style of exalting academicians and artists to places of power. James Roche, president of General Motors, never went to college, nor did many other top executives. Walter Reuther, one of our greatest natural leaders, had trouble with written tests and was a college dropout, leaving the cloister to build a powerful union of industrial workers. Harry Truman was not a college man.

Carl Schurz wrote about Lincoln, "I grant that he lacks higher education and his manners are not in accord with European conceptions of the dignity of a chief magistrate. He is a well-developed child of nature and is not skilled in polite phrases and poses. But he is a man of profound feeling, correct and firm principles and incorruptible honesty. His motives are unquestionable and he possesses to a remarkable degree the characteristic, God-given trait of this people, sound common sense."

Such measures of men have carried more weight in the selection of elites (at least of those not born to privilege) than measures of academic aptitude. Performance and energy have counted more in selecting top leaders than ability to take written examinations. That elites are now taken increasingly from among honor students may not invigorate our leadership.

Some American men of inherited, as well as earned, status (the Kennedys, Rockefellers, etc.) have been educated in all-male schools, and exposed to male societies when young. While sex segregation can be as bad as racism, boys can at least escape from mother figures in the all-male school. Such schools may breed sexual inversion as British boarding schools apparently do; but some American prep schools clearly avoid the sadism, Spartan rigors, and snobbery that seem to stimulate inversion in British prep schools. Other males of the elite avoid feminization by pursuing a passionate interest in tough sports and a committed and disciplined style of life.

The present power elites, furthermore, are recruits from a different society—from a rural or small-town, rather than urban or suburban, way of life. On the farm, males can more easily be men. The farm boy does useful and manly work at the side of his father. He is free to wander, without fear or urban perils. He is close to nature and the ways of men. His father is home and his mother is busy with a large family—weaving, sewing, gardening, ironing, washing by hand, baking bread, milking cows, feeding chickens—without any idle time to lavish on the cultivation of her sons. Many men in current power elites grew up in rural settings, but those of the future will more often come from the city's or suburb's feminized hothouses. . . .

One group of male intellectuals—college students—is in open rebellion against the academic abuses of intellect. Coeds have joined, but the uprising is led by boys. A submerged motive for this rebellion, as I have suggested before, is the college male's growing sense of having been duped and feminized by tasks assigned him in school.

As for the masculine boys, many of them have lost their struggle with the school and given up. Only a few become writers or researchers, or otherwise find effective ways to express opinions at all. Men who had trouble in school tend to blame themselves rather than the system and regret not having knuckled under. Most think their trouble in school is merely attributable to their own bad attitudes, and to no flaw in the school. They want only that their sons should not follow their own evil ways. Typically these men stay far away from the schools, take no part in them, and are often extremely hostile to student dissenters (for example, when there is a confrontation between the police and college demonstrators). As a rule, their only suggestions are that schools should teach more "vocational" subjects, have more work-study programs, and impose much more *effective* discipline. Beyond this useful contribution, they are silent.

If most men are out of the game, what about women? Many young girls grow fond of feminized males in school. In fact, a subtle but potent force is activated when women are exposed only to school values, and confined to women's work. Girls come to favor the kinds of boys who are honored in school, those who have ingested female values and who excel at word usage, fancy writing, and familiarity with the latest fashions in ideas and styles. As girls go, so go boys (though, of course, the reverse is also often true). If girls like football heroes, the boys will go out for the team. If they like brush cuts, boys will clip their hair. If girls prefer long hair, softness, ruffles, and boys with a taste for "culture," many boys will surely desert their barbers and their old rugged ways. *Cherchez la femme.*

The school shapes fashions in boys. If the school honored the masculine boy, so would girls. As it is, girls have but small chance in school to become familiar with anyone but other girls and feminized boys. Girls are expected to be good at art and the use of words, so they are often thrown together with only those boys who also lean toward these studies. There is no place where girls may, for example, share the boy's interest in technical and manual skills. There are few points of contact. Thus girls come to prefer, or at least to like, what is near-at-hand and familiar—

the feminized male. If schools more often put girls with masculine boys (in technological and other courses), many girls might lose the fear they have of such boys.

Subteen boys resist being feminized because they are uninterested in girls, if not openly hostile to them. Also, girls of this age are not yet much interested in "the arts." But older girls, influenced by teachers and the novels they read, have a more profoundly feminizing influence on the boys who have begun to follow them. (The all-male school has the unmistakable advantage of avoiding the feminizing influence of coeds, but it also has clear *dis*advantages which will be discussed later.)

Many women feel very strongly about the emasculation of men. They want men to be real men—at least *adult* women do (while many young girls are often afraid of real men, and do not yet see the need for strength as a survival tool). Mature women want men to be strong enough to stand up under the heavy burden of ordinary living. They want men to be strong so that women may safely be more assertive; as it is, many women feel they must restrain their own aggression and conceal their ability in order to stay in the man's shadow. Women also want men to be strong because strong men are more attractive and easier to respect over the long haul. Some women in the academy are uneasy about the quantities of feminized men and strong women found there. If they stay in the academy, they may not notice the difference, but if they go into the real world they may see a striking contrast with the men in the educational world.

All this is very thin ice to walk on so heavily. The delicacy or complexity of making observations and generalizations about masculinity cannot be exaggerated or overlooked. Still I must honestly report the striking neutral-to-feline nature of many males who function in educational institutions and related spheres. Some seem almost neuter in gender. Many others have a rather feline quality, a personality trait commonly ascribed to women. Many others are "nice boys" and "mama's boys" gone bad. It is as if they had always submitted, done what they were told, kept nice and clean, and loved mother—then suddenly they come into positions of great authority in the classroom. Now they can release all their contained rebellion, arrogance, and urge to be undisputed authorities. They act up, like spoiled children. They say whatever comes into their heads, no matter how malicious. They become the little Caesars mama wanted them to be. They do not have to be "nice" ever again. Some of them (especially in the field of literature) will bite and scratch their rivals—verbally, of course—and otherwise conduct their disputes in a way commonly ascribed to women. They are narcissistic, egocentric, spoiled, the screamers and scratchers, the bad boys among feminized males.

But the common garden variety of feminized male usually lacks this flamboyance and arrogance. Instead he is afflicted by excessive caution and a virtual incapacity to *do* anything in the real world—to have contact with all the dirt out there. With this type, appearances are especially deceiving. Cautious and fearful people will often act like bulls to shield their real nature. Hence we find that some of the most hawkish views on war and peace as well as the most dovish, are held by the feminized man. The dove in hawk's clothing, straining to make the masquerade a reality, is a common and dangerous presence on the international scene. And some of the worst violence in our cities occurs when men are reduced to carrying picket signs that insist: "I *am* a Man." . . .

## THE REVENGE OF WOMEN

Having excelled as scholars in the schools, girls then confront some of life's realities. In this society and most others, the stark reality is that men hold title to the best jobs, almost all the power, and most of the privilege and status that really count. It is indeed a man's world. As impotent feminists assert from time to time, women—a clear majority of the population—are treated by the working world as shabbily as some of our most dispossessed minorities.

So the first become the last. Those who start off fast in the public schools fall behind in the home stretch. Though more women than men graduate from high school, that is the end of female privilege. For the men who stay in the system, the rewards are abundant. Far more men enter college, and even more, relative to women, graduate. Far more men prepare for and get the best jobs. Girls win many more high school honors, but as soon as they enter college they fall behind. In its first year of operation, for example, Merit Scholarships—the most coveted college awards—were won by 400 boys and 150 girls. In 1966 boys won 65 percent of the Merit awards. Since girls are less likely to be urged to study math and science in high school, they are handicapped in most college competitions that require strong preparation in these fields. James Bryant Conant and others have deplored the fact that able girls are very underrepresented in high school math and science courses, and that in only 11 percent of high schools were girls taking what Conant regarded as an adequate program in these studies. It is assumed that girls cannot, or should not, compete in these fields, and girls accept the assumption.

The place of woman has traditionally been in the home. The German hausfrau, as we know, was assigned to *Kinder, Küche, Kirche*—children, kitchen, and church. In the twentieth century, the modern woman has been let out for some limited purposes. She has been admitted to the schools to work with children, and she has entered offices and factories to do clerical and other menial jobs.

The *Kinder* role to which she has been assigned, and her fierce domination of home and school, has tended to feminize the men she brings up. Hence, although the exclusion of women from "man's work" has protected certain male privileges, it has also left some unintended marks on men.

As a corollary to this, the exclusion of women from the "power structure" of the society—all the places where important decisions are made—has tended to dehumanize and sterilize most of our social institutions and seriously degrade the quality of our lives.

The institutions of our society are not in the hands of the most competent people. That is why most of them are so poorly run. The fact that women are rarely found in high office—in the school or anywhere else—is proof enough that the selection process is poor and biased.

Quite simply, what we must do is masculinize the schools and feminize the power structure of the society—balancing out the sexes so they don't corrode any one spot where they concentrate. A new balance would also familiarize women with the real world and give them the courage they need to confront it in their roles as trainers of the young. They cannot teach their sons and students much about the world when they themselves live in total ignorance of it.

The home is woman's private domain, but it is not always big enough for her. Her lavished energies fill the house and overflow it. There, in lieu of genuine self-realization she may turn her full effort to the indulgence, domination, and even seduction of her sons. Since few women can sustain such extravagant intimacy, many alternate between love and hostility, giving the anxious impression to their sons that mother may be more antagonist than protector. Such women also will usually guard their sons from roughneck play, dirt, conflict, body contact, or even normal active play with friends.

While the sons of such mothers may do very well in school and the academy, they are often retarded in normal masculine growth and are found everywhere in conflict with themselves or others. They swell the ranks of the alienated, the withdrawn or rejected, the fearful, the addicted, the feminized.

Psychologist David Levy found that overprotective mothers kept their sons from playing with others and forming close friendships. They gratified their son's whims, fondled them, slept with them until they often were almost grown, and otherwise infantilized them. These boys excelled in school, had large vocabularies and high IQs, and their major interest was in reading. They were poor in sports and social relations. They were afraid of other children and liked to play with girls. They behaved well in school, but so miserably at home that their mothers felt they could no longer manage them. Typically, they were tyrannical and extremely messy, expecting their mothers always to clean up after them. These indulged children were taller and heavier than the "controls" (other children their age) but not adept or interested in physical activity or skill.

Those with dominating mothers had even more trouble becoming men than those with mothers who were simply indulgent. In only one case in this study did a mother work. Her son was the only one who was able to achieve (in his mother's absence from home) normal relations with other boys!

Women who enjoy a satisfying sex life and are normally devoted to their husbands will not be excessively involved with their sons, the study concludes. Those who work will also be unlikely to devote themselves with such ferocity to the protection and domination of their sons.

Based on such evidence, it is clear that consignment of women to child-rearing in the home and school can, and perhaps often does, result in the emasculation of the boys who come under their control. Of course, most women who stay close to home are more benign and less domineering than those of the Levy study. Inevitably, however, a good deal of the mother's female temperament is bound to rub off on her son when the two spend much time together. If the mother herself has been raised, as many have, to be rather submissive and fearful, these qualities are likely as well to be transmitted to sons. We might then argue for a more vigorous training of girls so that they will be able to pass along more assertive qualities to sons. Indeed, such is the rationale behind the education of women in developing societies. If the mother is educated, she will pass her training on to her sons. If she is taught to seek the new and useful and to abandon obsolete traditions, she will transmit this progressive mood to her offspring. If women are encouraged to be timid and accepting rather than assertive and independent they will surely raise fearful sons. . . .

Many women actively dislike and resent males. They take their revenge where they can, in the home and the school, on the young males they control. They both pamper them and punish them. The solution is to remove boys from the sole jurisdiction of women, and to correct the social injustices that make many women so resentful of men.

Mama is only half the problem. The other half is Papa. Papa's absence from home, his abdication of authority to Mama, his weakness, brutality, or failure to relate to his son can also lead to feminization. Because so many fathers—among the rich, as among the poor—are deficient in one way or another, father substitutes are needed in the schools to give boys a strong taste of what it's like to be an adequate adult male.

While women enjoy certain privileges—inherited wealth and status and minor courtesies from men—they are disinherited with respect to *earned* status and many things that really count. They are openly excluded from all seats of social power. While they are kept from some of the heaviest physical labor, they are also excluded from some of the most satisfying. They *obey*, rather than *make*, rules and laws. Expected to show minor talent and make minor decisions, they live up to expectations with surprising good will. When more is expected, they are equally accommodating.

Women control *none* of the institutions in the society. They have great influence in home, school, and church—too much—but even these institutions are governed by men: the "head" of the house, the superintendent of schools, the church hierarchy. They may leave most of the work and the daily operations to women, but men are the masters. The servility of women is most extreme in those ancient religions which still keep old masters in modern houses—men that live off the patronage of women but permit them no place in their clergies or hierarchies, except to govern other women or children.

## SUGGESTED READINGS

Carol Andreas, *Sex and Caste in America,* Englewood Cliffs: Prentice-Hall, 1971. Presents data to argue that the educational and family systems in our society hardly feminize men, but instead push men into a rigid masculine role (and women into a feminine one).

Myron Brenton, *The American Male,* New York: Fawcett, 1967. Argues that men suffer too for the separation of sex roles in our society, but rejects the idea of "masculinity" that Sexton presumes.

Helen Z. Lopata, *Occupation: Housewife,* New York: Oxford, 1971. The first large-scale study of housewives, which destroys the stereotype implicit in much social science writings that these women are passive, fearful, unimaginative, and clutching of their husbands or sons.

# Sex Differences in Game Strategy

Clarice Stasz Stoll and
Paul T. McFarlane

Many scholars prefer to use an experimental approach whenever possible because it enables them to control the social environment and thus test their ideas in a pure, if unreal, situation. This study is a small addition to a long series of small-groups investigations. In the early 1950's it was discovered that small groups often develop two distinctive types of leaders, one concerned with task accomplishment, the other with the emotional life of the members. Typically, males would be found to be task oriented and females people oriented. Similarly, males would exhibit competitive behavior while females would be accommodating. The males' behavior has been described at times as more "rational" because it is goal-oriented. Or so it would appear.

This small-groups literature is important because of its implications for other social groups. For example, some of this research led to theories about the American family (see Suggested Readings) emphasizing the traditional definition of male and female roles. Although later research on families produced data that did not agree with these theories, their acceptance continues. In fact, there has even been a tendency to argue that the sex role difference *should* be perpetuated because it has been shown to exist—whether in experiments or in the minds of theorists.

---

From *Sociometry*, Vol. 32, 3, September, 1969, pp. 259-272. Reprinted with permission of the authors and the American Sociological Association.

We undertook the following study partly because of some evidence in the experimental literature that women are not necessarily less competitive than men. Also, we used a cooperative game as a way of determining how "rationally" men would behave in a noncompetitive situation. The results suggest that traditional views about sex differences are oversimplified. The data also show how sex roles can confound one's chance for success in life, although in this case the males were the losers because their competitive efforts went unrewarded.

In the western world life is competitive. Suppose that future social change moved toward a more cooperative social structure. Given our study, would you expect women to be more successful? Your response depends on whether you believe males to be "innately" competitive, and whether you think that it is possible and advisable to generalize from a study like this.

Can you see any other analogues between this game and real life? Is it reasonable to argue from our data that the male sex role in American society is more rigidly defined than the female? How could you test this (or the opposing) hypothesis? Finally, do you see how this study could be used for political purposes by both those in favor and those against policies that break down sexist practices?

---

One of the few theoretical statements on game situations is Goffman's essay "Fun in Games" (1961). Goffman's theory is eminently sociological in that he is concerned with the social characteristics of players, their combined effects upon the game process, and the resulting meaning of the situation for players. Notably, he does not treat games *in vacuo*, but views them in spatial-temporal dimensions. As a result, he views games as situations which can be entered into with various degrees of role involvement. "Spontaneous involvement"—the degree to which a player treats the game as serious—forms the focal point of Goffman's discussion on games.

The best predictor of how a person will take to a game, Goffman suggests, is the degree to which there is an alignment between external variables and games variables. There must be consistency in the transition from one's real life situation to the game situation. This simple idea is fruitful for numerous hypotheses concerning games. For example, one might predict that females in authority roles in games will be less engrossed in the game or less comfortable with their situation. Or, that in a game with a hierarchy of statuses, an isomorphism of player's social status outside the game with the status inside the game would optimize player involvement.

To the degree that a player is not engrossed in the game he will demonstrate role distance. The major thrust of Goffman's essay is to discuss the ways in which groups respond to signs of disengagement and prevent a permanent disruption of the game. Thus, the very course of the game is influenced by individual adjustments to the game role and group responses to these individual adjustments. The question of interest here then is to what extent do external roles of the participants contribute to the development of strategy?

## SEX DIFFERENCES IN GAMES

Goffman urges us to interpret behavior in terms of its meaning for the ambient as well as immediate situation. Yet he leaves important questions unanswered. One problem is how to decide which roles are likely to affect game involvement. Are only *visible* roles relevant, for instance? A second question is whether games can be typed such that one could predict the relevance of certain external roles for games. For example would all games with a hierarchy of roles be affected by the same external characteristics such as status or sex? Then there is the possibility that some roles are always relevant, no matter what the structure of the game. One reasonable hypothesis here is that ascribed characteristics would strongly influence game process when all players are strangers to one another. Finally, there is the possibility that some extra-game roles become relevant as the game develops. Thus being a female in a mixed-sex competition may not emerge as inhibiting until the player moves to the top position.

These questions can be applied to the study of small group structure and process in general. For this reason the small groups literature was examined for studies of external role and group process. The paucity of investigations on this topic was noted in three major reviews of the field. Golembiewski (1962) treats the effects of individual members upon the group solely in terms of personality differences, with no reference to social characteristics. His oversight is not unreasonable. For as Hare (1962:206-224) has noted, the social characteristics of group members are usually "held constant" in research because they are so easy to control. McGrath and Altman's review (1966) identified many biographical characteristics distinguishing the samples in research. These variables cover a range from sex or age to weight and region of birth. Still, their intensive survey of a sample of 250 studies representative of the small-groups literature located only 32 in which any relationship between biographical characteristics and some group variable was examined. Among the 32 studies were:

> . . . no cases of tests for association between biographical characteristics and various properties of the group and interpersonal relations within the group . . . with content, patterns and outcomes of member interaction, nor with several measures of group performance effectiveness. (106-107)

At least two social characteristics have received systematic attention. First, child study literature (by definition) has considerable data on age-status and children's social behavior. (See Hare, 1962:206-208.) More important for our purposes is the research on sex role. A number of studies on sex-role and behavior in discussion groups has shown that females are more reactive and display agreement, while males are more active or antagonistic. (For example, Strodtbeck and Mann, 1956.)

There has also been a cumulation of data on sex differences in game situations. Certain consistencies are found across studies of sex differences in negotiation behavior. Explanations for the findings are less in agreement. From his studies of females in triad games, Vinacke (1959; also Uesugi and Vinacke, 1963) concludes that feminine strategy is "accommodative," while masculine strategy is "exploitative." Data from other studies (Borah, 1963; Shomer's study as reported in Kelley, 1965) of an interdependency game, the Trucking Game, have revealed that females will utilize techniques to avoid competitive encounters. Males not only enter into direct encounters more readily, but also spend more time in standoffs. The above investigators usually interpret the results as a reflection on the female's part to avoid competition or to perform integrative functions.

In contrast, Joseph and Willis (1963) have suggested that females are more differentiated in terms of aggressivenesss or competitiveness. Males are more consistently aggressive across situations. Rapaport and Chammah's (1966) data on Prisoner's Dilemma support this view (although they make no reference to it). Females displayed fewer cooperative responses than males. However, females were also more likely to react to opponent's preemption by an act of appeasement. Males were more consistently steadfast. Hence females are not necessarily more cooperative or less aggressive. They appear, rather, to differentiate a competitive situation into a dominant-subordinate relationship.

These findings suggest that sex is a better predictor of individual male behavior than female in a competitive situation. Males will enter and perpetuate stalemates. Females may enter stalemates as frequently, but one opponent will readily retreat or make overtures of appeasement. From Goffman's perspective, the competition is role-expressive for males. Competition apparently does not intrude upon femininity, at least that of American college sophomores.

The literature on sex-role in negotiation games suggests a general principle: external roles are relevant for games to the extent that game moves have meaning for expression of the roles. Wherever alternatives are available, players will opt for choices which maintain their definitions of their extra-game roles, even though the game structure might not reward such moves.

## THE PARENT-CHILD SIMULATION

An existing simulation game, Parent-Child, was chosen as the research instrument. This is a game which simulates the relationship between a parent and an adolescent child originally developed by Boocock and Schild (1969). The original version of the game was employed in the research reported in this section of the present report.

Parent-Child is a two-person, non-zero-sum game with a cooperative solution. It is played by two subjects face-to-face, with one person taking the role of parent, and the other the role of child. Neither role is specified with respect to sex.

The structure of the game is as follows. There is a board listing five issues on which the parent and child have opposing attitudes. For example, on one issue, the parent wants the child to be home by 10 o'clock; the child wants to be able to stay out later. On each issue point cards are randomly distributed on each player's side, making the issues worth 2, 4, 6, 8, or 10 points, respectively. Due to this random allocation of points, the parent and child may have similar or different point values for each of the issues.

The game is interesting sociologically in that rounds are separated into two phases. There is first a discussion stage during which the dyad members must communicate directly with one another in order to establish a definition of the situation, i.e., the specific norms of behavior for the child. Any variables which could affect the players' interaction and, in particular, their ability to reach a consensus about the issues would be relevant for predicting outcomes at this stage of the game. The measure of consensus attained by a dyad is simply the number of agreements made on the issues. One of the working hypotheses of the study was then that player characteristics which would facilitate interaction would result in ability to reach agreements on the issues.

During the second stage each player acts individually in turn. The child acts first, by behaving in accordance with the agreements or in disobedience of parental orders. The child can earn all the points by simply acting according to the way he defines issues as important. However, if he has broken an agreement or an order at any point, he will face possible punishment from the parent. The optimal strategy is for the players to develop trust such that agreements are made in favor of both players, that the child does not break the agreements, and that the parent will not punish maximally in case of minor disobedience.

Social characteristics could affect progress toward the rational strategy in two basic ways. First, they may facilitate the development of consensus during the discussion phase. This part of the game is typically characterized by rich, dramatic role-play in which players give excuses or accounts for not submitting to the other's will. Agreements appear to be related to a common definition as to what accounts are reasonable. (For more on accounts and interaction, see Scott and Lyman, 1968.) To the extent that players have dissimilar social characteristics, we would expect difficulties in establishing common grounds.

During the phase when each player acts individually in expression of his role, the meaning of certain choices for the maintenance of definitions external to the game is most relevant. For example, we would expect threats to be made to the degree that they are expressive of definitions external to the game. Interestingly, social characteristics which aid in the development of consensus (e.g., all male) may impede role-expression conducive to a cooperative strategy.

Players' displays of strength will be the result of more than the meaning of activities for external game definitions. Child's decision to disobey will be affected by the number of agreements he gets in his favor. Similarly, parent's decision to punish will be influenced by the degree of disobedience. More importantly, each player will look to the way in which the other kept trust or provided reciprocity. If child decreases the amount of disobedience, yet parent continues to punish strictly and severely, then child is unlikely to continue in face of lack of reciprocity. Accordingly, if parent makes the initial appeasing move and weakens his punishment, we should not expect him to remain lenient if child continues to disobey.

To summarize the model: development towards the optimal strategy would be reflected by (1) few issuances of orders; (2) low probability of disobedience; (3) low probability of punishment; (4) low amount of punishment. The likelihood of reaching agreements will be affected by the players' ability to interact smoothly and reach a common definition of the situation. Players' individual responses in terms of obedience and punishment are likely to be a function of both the degree of consensus and one's partner's behavior in prior rounds. Thus there will be a cumulative development of actions toward the rational strategy or towards impeding its development.

## METHODOLOGY

*Study Design and Sample.* The research was administered at a virtually all-black high school in a large city. The game was introduced in seven 10th and 11th grade English classes as part of their regular curriculum. Students in these classes were generally below average on achievement test performance and were deficient in reading skills.

Parent-Child was administered for three consecutive days by a team of field workers. A total of 158 students participated. The sample base here is much smaller, consisting of 66 students. These students are those who played three full games (beyond practice round) with the same partner, in the same game role, filling out score sheets with apparent accuracy. Sample attrition resulted partly from absenteeism (which meant eliminating any partners of the absentee student) and from failure to complete three full games.

The game score sheets were devised to compute the following: (1) number of agreements favoring parent and child each; (2) number of orders (which added to (1) sums to five); (3) probability of disobedience, a ratio of actual to potential deviance; (4) probability of punishment, a ratio of actual to potential punishment; (5) mean punishment, which ranges from 0 to 7 points.

*Hypothesis.* The following prediction was made:

That female dyads will more likely use the rational strategy than male dyads.

Given that the rational strategy is a cooperation-appeasement one, previous research on games suggests that females will adopt this solution. (To what extent we can say they "learned" the solution is another question.)

*Dyad Composition and Rationality.* For clarity's sake the data are presented in graphical form, as well as tabular form. The graphs are presented in order of game moves—agreements, orders, disobedience, punishment, assignment of punishment severity—to facilitate tracing through how sequence of moves develops. Recognizing both that agreements and orders come out of the discussion period, and that other moves are individually determined assists in interpreting reasons for the game process. It can then be understood how the process of development toward the rational strategy takes several paths.

According to the hypothesis, we expect females to reach the rational solution more readily than males. Although female dyads do move toward a more cooperative strategy than male dyads, it is not simply because females are more accommodative and males more exploitative.

From the data in Figure 1, it can be seen that female dyads begin Round 1 less coordinated than male dyads. Females order more in Round 1 (2.44 to 1.41) and have a higher probability of disobedience than males (.66 to .50). The differentiating point in the comparative development toward rationality is parent's behavior. Female parents punish moderately (5.04) what is frequent disobedience, while male parents punish more severely (6.84) what is moderate disobedience.

In Round 2, female dyads show increasing cooperation in their increased number of agreements (2.00) and decreased number of orders (1.73). Probability of disobedience decreased slightly in the second round (from .66 to .61), as does probability of punishment (.90 to .81). In addition, the average number of points of punishment for female dyad decreased from Round 1 to Round 2 (5.04 to 4.88).

The male dyads do not show these increases in rationality and/or cooperation over time. Only in probability of punishment and in the average number of points of punishment do the male dyads show movement toward the rational strategy. It appears that the initial show of strength in all male dyads, as evidenced by their probability of punishment scores (1.00) and average number of points of punishment scores (6.84) in the first round resulted in a situation inimical to cooperation.

Table 1 Mean game scores by dyad sex composition

| | Male dyads | Female dyads |
|---|---|---|
| 1. Agreements to parent | | |
| Round 1 | 1.58 (12) | 1.56 (16) |
| Round 2 | 2.00 (12) | 2.00 (20) |
| Round 3 | 1.25 (12) | 1.85 (20) |
| 2. Number of orders | | |
| Round 1 | 1.41 (12) | 2.44 (16) |
| Round 2 | 1.44 (12) | 1.73 (20) |
| Round 3 | 2.25 (12) | 1.86 (21) |
| 3. Probability of disobedience | | |
| Round 1 | .50 (12) | .66 (21) |
| Round 2 | .42 (12) | .61 (21) |
| Round 3 | .52 (12) | .54 (20) |
| 4. Probability of punishment | | |
| Round 1 | 1.00 (10) | .90 (19) |
| Round 2 | .90 (8) | .81 (17) |
| Round 3 | .86 (9) | .75 (16) |
| 5. Average punishment | | |
| Round 1 | 6.84 (10) | 5.04 (18) |
| Round 2 | 6.54 (7) | 4.88 (18) |
| Round 3 | 6.04 (7) | 5.33 (15) |

Total Number of all-male dyads = 12
all-female dyads = 21

The findings thus replicate Rapaport and Chammah's results on feminine strategy in Prisoner's Dilemma. Females tend to differentiate roles in competitive situations, while males do not. The results are interesting in view of three divergences from the Rapaport-Chammah design. First, the females are biographically unlike the white, high achievement, college students used in previous studies. Secondly, there was no face-to-face interaction in Prisoner's Dilemma. Finally, the problem was immersed in the social context of parent-child relationship. It can be concluded accordingly that the sex differences found in previous studies are not idiosyncratic to the typical experimental situation. Also, the addition of face-to-face interaction does not change the differential development of strategy. Finally, the parent-child context does not reshape or provide additions to the structure of the dilemma situation.

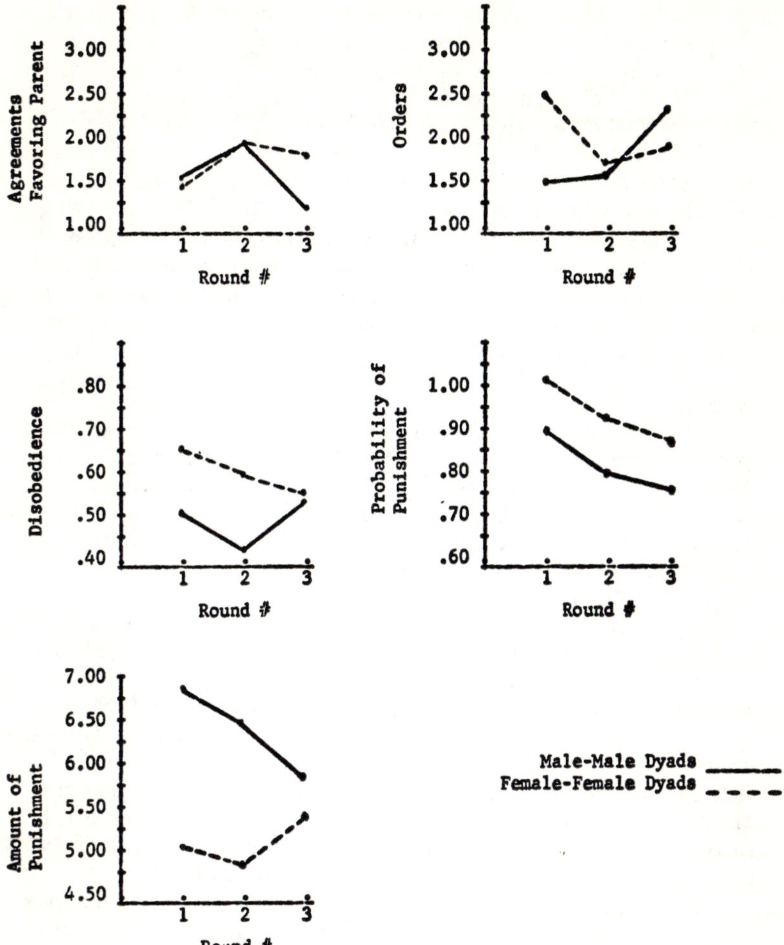


Figure 1 Mean game scores by dyad sex composition

## SUMMARY AND IMPLICATIONS

Entering a game is entering a new social order. Players face one another as actors-in-roles that are defined through the rules. In working toward the goal of the game, the player learns the system of rules and must adapt to other players' actions within this system of rules. As in real life, players do not enter the situation free to slip simply into the cloak of the assigned roles. Instead, they still bear signs of other statuses with their accompanying obligations. This study examined some of the ways in which external characteristics penetrated into game activity. The results help us to understand why there is great variability in social activity across sets of interactions with the same structure and purpose.

The data suggest that performing the role of "player-trying-to-win" may be subverted or superseded by external characteristics. The expression of masculine role behavior mitigated against taking a cooperative stance in the game, *even though the game highly rewarded cooperation.* On the other hand, females were able to respond consistently and more facilely within the player roles. Normality and individual success in these cases may have been achieved unintentionally.

The consistency of these findings on sex differences with those of previous experiments is clearly the major finding. To date studies of sex differences in negotiation settings has utilized college students (presumably white) in experimental settings with simple laboratory games. In this study the subjects were younger, black, and low-academic performers who played a game of rich content in a familiar setting.

Unlike much experimental research in which groups are loosely organized around discussion or trivial tasks, games provide a controlled structure from their onset. Through the former type of group it is possible to study structural development and differentiation. There are, however, many groups in society not composed of strangers with shortrun goals. Rather, they are well-ordered with complex aims. Games are a most suitable environment for studying behavior in such groups, particularly such topics as role learning, the operation of formal control mechanisms, the development of informal relations in task groups, and so forth.

Finally, a subtle point which is often overlooked in analyses is suggested by these data. Although researchers often control along relevant subject characteristics, in the very act of controlling along these dimensions they ignore important process differences. For example, investigators will run an experiment separately for males and females, and, on the basis of cross-sex comparisons of outcome measures will decide that males and females are either alike or different. This is a reasonable procedure, but the conclusion assumes that the conceptual or behavior processes of the two groups are identical. Had we analyzed our data this way, e.g., looked only at third round results, we may well have concluded that there were not large sex differences. In fact the behavioral responses within groups over time were quite dissimilar. To conclude, when experimenters find it necessary to control on subject social characteristics, they should not ignore the possibility of process differences not revealed by output differences.

## REFERENCES

Boocock, Sarane S. and E. O. Schild, *Parent-Child*, New York: Western, 1969.

Borah, L. A., Jr., "The effects of threat in bargaining: critical and experimental analysis." *Journal of Abnormal and Social Psychology* **66** (January 1963): 181-189.

Goffman, Erving, *Encounters*. Indianapolis: Bobbs-Merrill, 1961.

Golembiewski, Robert T., *The Small Group*. Chicago: University of Chicago, 1962.

Hare, A. Paul, *Handbook of Small Group Research*. New York: Free Press, 1962.

Joseph, M. L. and R. H. Willis, "An experimental analog to two-party bargaining." *Behavioral Science* **8** (April 1963): 117-127.

Kelley, Harold H., "Experimental studies of threats in interpersonal negotiations." *Journal of Conflict Resolution* **9** (March 1965): 79-105.

McGrath, Joseph E. and Irwin Altman, *Small Group Research*. New York: Holt, Rinehart, and Winston, 1966.

Rapaport, Anatol and Albert M. Chammah, "The game of chicken." *American Behavioral Scientist* **10** (November 1966): 10-28.

Scott, Marvin B. and Stanford M. Lyman, "Accounts." *American Sociological Review* **33** (February 1968): 46-62.

Strodtbeck, Fred L. and Richard D. Mann, "Sex role differentiation in jury deliberations." *Sociometry* **19** (March 1956): 3-11.

Usuegi, Thomas K. and W. Edgar Vinacke, "Strategy in a feminine game." *Sociometry* **26** (December 1963): 75-88.

Vinacke, W. Edgar, "Sex roles in the three-person game." *Sociometry* **22** (March 1959): 343-360.

## SUGGESTED READINGS

Blood, Robert O., Jr, and Donald M. Wolfe, *Husbands and Wives,* New York: Free Press, 1960. A study of families in the Detroit area, which presents evidence contradicting many assumptions about the typical American family.

Parsons, Talcott, and Robert F. Bales, *Family, Socialization, and Interaction Process,* New York: Free Press, 1955. Elaborates a theory of nuclear family organization premised upon a rigid sex role differentiation.

Seward, Georgene H., and Robert C. Williamson, *Sex Roles in Changing Society,* New York: Random House, 1970. A collection of essays by specialists on various cultures that documents both the traditional sex roles and the changes that are occurring in recent years.

Skolnick, Arlene S., and Jerome H. Skolnick, *Families in Transition,* Boston: Little, Brown, 1971. Provocative papers that question the model of marriage prevalent in social science literature, with a consideration of new forms of family life and child-rearing.

# Women in Labor

Marijean Suelzle

No volume on sexism would be complete without a descriptive study on sexually based discrimination in our own society. Such papers constitute the major theme of feminist literature. Marijean Suelzle's survey of women in the labor force is exceptional in that she works with statistical data to provide a coherent picture of pervasive discrimination. It is not difficult to see why some feminists argue that females are twentieth-century slaves. In addition, Suelzle uses her materials well to dispel some of the cliches brought forth to prove that women have no reason to complain about their lot.

Where do these myths come from? Not from men only – current national polls reveal that the majority of women subscribe to similar notions. As with other minority groups, women have accepted the stereotypes about themselves and act within the restrictions of these definitions.

In trying to defeat these myths, however, Suelzle may be accused of perpetuating some of the male-dominant values. Must everyone, men and women, be committed to the concept of a career, for example? Her position is defensive when she assumes that being a good worker as defined by the employer is important. Hence her article will probably appeal more to those who are in favor of using a "general welfare" approach to end sex discrimination.

---

Suelzle's recommendations for change reflect this view, with her emphasis upon the need for day-care centers, women in apprenticeship programs, removal of protective labor laws, and so forth. Yet she notes that whatever jobs men do are the ones defined as important, the ones that get the high rewards. If her proposals were put in practice, how do we know that men wouldn't again shift their jobs or redefine the situation to reestablish the present status quo? Hence are Suelzle's proposals sufficient to bring about the end of sexism?

Those who have a Marxist point of view will argue that Suelzle's suggestions are patchwork solutions because she does not propose to change the society's total value system, with its emphasis on technology, economic efficiency, and status display. What recommendations for change would you make were you to accept this latter position? Do any of Suelzle's data give credence to this point of view?

---

To read the newspapers one would think that the top jobs in public life are opening up for women and that our occupational status was rising generally: Interstate Commerce Commissioner Virginia Mae Brown became the first woman to head an independent federal administrative agency; Helen D. Bentley became chairman of the Maritime Commission; the first four female scientists explored the Antarctic; Barbara J. Rubin, a jockey, was the first woman to win a pari-mutuel race; and a 13-year-old girl, Alice DeRivera, integrated the all-male Stuyvesant High School in New York. While publicity on the "breakthroughs" does break down some psychological barriers, it exaggerates and misrepresents the real occupational changes. In order to find out what these real changes are, we must look at social trends that affect the changing profile of women in the labor force and at some myths and stereotypes that surround the working woman.

In 1920 the average woman worker in this country was 28 years old and single. Today she is 39 years old, married and living with her husband. In 1920 she was most likely to be a factory worker or other operative, but large numbers of women were also clerical workers, private household workers and farm workers. Her occupational choice was extremely limited. Today the average woman in the labor force is most likely to be a clerical worker, with other large numbers of women being service workers outside the home, factory workers or other operatives and professional or technical workers. She may be working in any one of 479 individual occupations, but most women are concentrated in a relatively small number of occupations.

## TIMES OF LIFE AND WORK

Caroline Bird has identified five factors influencing the changing profile of the woman worker. First, the vital statistics of birth, marriage and death have changed so that women have more years of life when they are not bearing or rearing children. One of the most important factors effecting the change is greater longevity, especially for women. The baby girl born in 1900 (that is, the grandmother of many women entering the labor force today) had a life expectancy of 48 years, whereas the baby girl born today has a life expectancy of 74 years, a figure that can be expected to go higher. About half today's women marry by age 20, and more marry at age 18 than at any other age. On the average, they will have had their last child by age 30 and will be in their mid-thirties by the time their youngest child is in school. The mother will have about 40 years, or one-half, of her life ahead of her, freed from child-rearing responsibilities.

A second important factor affecting the profile of the woman worker is education. Girls have consistently outnumbered boys among high school graduates, although the difference has narrowed. In 1900, girls were approximately 60 percent of all high school graduates, whereas recently the number of girls graduating from high school is only slightly higher than the number of boys—50.4 and 49.6 percent respectively in 1968. During this period, of course, the number of both girls and boys graduating from high school has been growing steadily. Each year more women enroll in and graduate from institutions of higher education, but women still lag behind men in pursuing education beyond high school, and, according to Dean Knudsen, the lag is *increasing*. Women earned 19 percent of the bachelor's or first professional degrees awarded in 1900, as against 41 percent in 1965; 19 percent of the master's degrees awarded in 1900, as against 32 percent in 1965; and 6 percent of the doctor's degrees awarded in 1900, as against 11 percent in 1965. But if we take the period 1940 to 1964 and asked what proportion of girls were enrolled for degree credit, Dean Knudsen has shown that the proportion of girls has declined by 5.5 percent.

A third factor is the experience of employment itself. In 1900, women were only 18 percent of all workers; in 1940, about

25 percent. The proportion reached a high of 36 percent during World War II, dropped back to 28 percent with the return of male veterans to civilian jobs, before beginning to climb again to 37 percent today. The shift in production from home to factory has influenced the rise in the numbers and proportion of women in the labor force. The work ethic, self-fulfillment and the right of each individual to happiness have increasingly become associated with educational and career attainment, the paycheck and its rate of increase. Thus, the homemaker role as the only role capable of meeting the cultural ideals is called into question. Far from a shameful necessity reflecting the inadequacy of the husband as provider, earnings have become a point of pride for wives of men who are obviously able to "support" them adequately.

A fourth minor factor affecting the profile of the woman worker is the increasing desegregation of work. Sex-typing of jobs, however, remains the norm. The woman worker is concentrated in a relatively small number of occupations. One-third of all working women are employed in seven occupations—secretary, saleswoman, general private household worker, teacher in elementary school, bookkeeper, waitress and professional nurse. This can be contrasted to the scarcity of women in such professional positions as physician, engineer, and scientist despite the increased job openings created by the tremendous interest in research and development. Job channeling and labeling come about through custom, an unquestioning acceptance of certain assumptions about masculinity and feminity. The question asked is often "Is it fitting and proper?" rather than "Is she qualified?"

The fifth and final factor affecting the profile of the woman worker is a general desegregation of the sexes—in the professions, the church, education, recreation and public accommodation.

To the above five factors identified by Caroline Bird, a sixth can be added, that of an increasing awareness of and concern over the population explosion. Although population predictions are necessarily tentative, Dr. Richard S. Miller, a Yale University ecologist, projects the current doubling time of the world's human population as 36 years, into the next century, 20 years beginning in 2000 and 16 years beginning in 2020. The total world population by his projection is 28 billion people in 2036, an obvious impossibility. Some women today are aware not only that motherhood is not enough but also that, for the first time in history, it is actually socially irresponsible to have as many children as one would like. The efforts of such social movements as Zero Population Growth, with their goal of one adult, one child, have already

Women and Careers

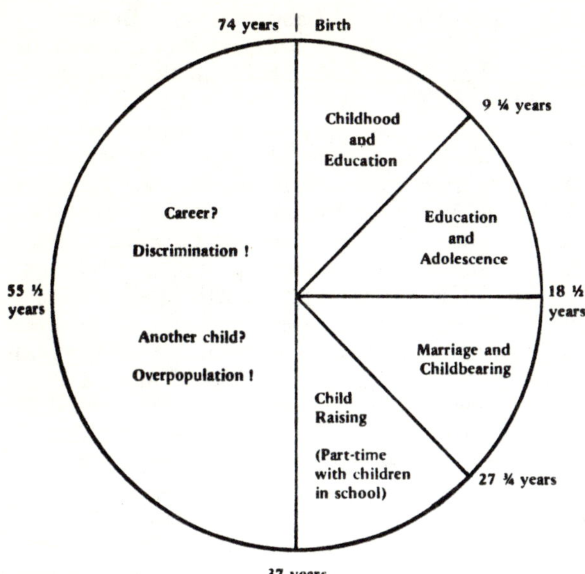


**Figure 1** The baby girl born in 1970 has a life expectancy of 74 years. About half of today's women marry by age 20, and more marry at age 18 than at any other age. On the average, they will have had their last child by age 30 and will be in their mid-thirties by the time their youngest child is in school. The mother will have about one-half of her life ahead of her. If she decides to reenter the job market after a period of absence for childrearing, she will face difficulty in upgrading her skills and discrimination in an occupational structure geared to continuous (male) employment. At the same time, an increased concern with the population explosion will influence her not to have more than two children.

caused some women to report negative social reactions when they are expecting their third (or more) child. Such social criticism is leading many women to seek career alternatives rather than bearing more than two (or in some cases any) children.

## CHANGING PROFILE OF WOMEN IN THE LABOR FORCE

According to the U. S. Department of Labor Women's Bureau, there have been some startling changes in the profile of women in the labor force, as there have been in the profile of the woman who actually works. However, the change have *not* all been unidirectional and do not bear out the "onward and upward ideology" reflected in the media. While the rate of labor force participation has expanded, earnings relative to males are down, as are the rates of women employed in most higher status occupations. Factors pushing and attracting women into the labor force are increasing while, at the same time, rewards for so participating are declining.

Fifty years ago, in 1920, less than one-fourth of all women 20 to 60 years of age in the population were workers (23 percent). Today almost half of all women 18 to 64 years of age in the population are workers (49 percent). The age at which women were most apt to be working has remained the same over the last 50 years although the rate has changed. During both periods women were most apt to be working at ages 20 to 24; but only 38 percent were working in January 1920, as opposed to 56 percent in April 1969. The pattern of employment throughout the life cycle has also changed. In 1920 female participation in the labor force dropped off at age 25, decreased steadily with age, and by the time they were aged 45 to 54 only 18 percent were working. In contrast, female participation in the labor force today drops off at age 25 but rises again at age 35 to a second peak of 54 percent at ages 45 to 54. The changed pattern of employment throughout the life cycle reflects the different employment outlook of the 35-year-old woman in 1920. In 1920 less than one out of every five women 35 to 64 years of age was in the labor force. Today almost half the women at age 35 can expect to work 24 to 31 more years. More than one-half of today's young women will work full-time for 25 or more years. Today 37 percent of all workers are women.

As I mentioned earlier, women are concentrated in a relatively small number of occupations. The number of occupations in which 100,000 or more women were employed increased between 1950 and the present time by the addition of seven occupations—baby-sitter, charwoman and cleaner, counter and fountain worker, file clerk, housekeeper (apart from private household) and stewardess, musician and music teacher and receptionist—hardly impressive additions when one bears in mind the increased educational attainment of women during this period.

Another example of the clear sex-typing of (underpriced)

"women's work" shows up if we examine sex ratios in the major occupational categories. In more than half of the 36 occupations in which 100,000 or more women were employed in 1960, at least three out of four workers were women; in at least one-third, nine out of ten were women.

Women have been gaining status in some sectors of the economy, but they have been losing it in others. For example, in the executive branch of the Federal Civilian Service, increasing numbers of young women are taking the Federal Service Entrance Examination and being appointed to professional positions at entrance levels. Their numbers have doubled between 1963 and 1967 (rising from 18 to 35 percent). In addition, 29 percent of those selected as management interns in 1967 were women, as compared to only 14 percent in 1965. At the same time, however, the proportion of women teachers at the college and university level has declined. Only 22 percent of the faculty and other professional staff in institutions of higher education were women in 1964, down from the proportion in 1940 (28 percent), 1930 (27 percent) or 1920 (26 percent).

When averages are computed separately for men and for women in the labor force, women are consistently shown to be the disadvantaged group. Women workers are concentrated in lower-paying jobs, they earn less than men in all kinds of jobs, and their unemployment rate is higher. Furthermore, the gap between the earnings of women and of men has been steadily widening since 1956 (see table). Thus, the status of women in the labor force relative to the status of men has been declining for at least the past 15 years. Furthermore, the areas in which women have been making positive occupational gains are more than being offset by those areas in which opportunities have been decreasing.

The increase in women's employment is a case of moving in, not up. Top positions for women are too few relative to their increased educational attainments over the past 50 years. There are many reasons for the pay and status differentials, most of them based on hoary stereotypes concerning women's work. But these attitudes and practices are fostered not only by the employer but the woman employee herself. For even though many of these myths have been shattered by serious investigation, there are few truths that make their way easily and quickly into public knowledge to become new myths. Some of the current myths are these:

**Myth 1: Women naturally don't want careers, they just want jobs.**

As a generalization about women entering or in the job market in 1970, the statement may or may not be accurate. It is a myth because of the "naturally." There is nothing natural about the low aspirations of women, any more than the low aspirations of ethnic minorities in public life. To assume that "ambition" is unfeminine is to admit no individual variability: it depends on the person, not the sex.

In a recent study Matina Horner administered a story completion test to female and male undergraduates. Women were asked to write a story based on the sentence "After first-term finals, Anne finds herself at the top of her medical-school class." (Men were given the same task, but with the word "John" replacing the word "Anne" in the sentence.) Over 65 percent of the girls told stories which reflected strong fears of social rejection, fears about definitions of womanhood or denial of the possibility that any mere woman could be so successful:

> Anne is pretty darn proud of herself, but everyone hates and envies her.
>
> Anne is pleased. She had worked extraordinarily hard, and her grades showed it. "It is not enough," Anne thinks. "I am not happy." She didn't even want to be a doctor. She is not sure what she wants. Anne says to hell with the whole business and goes into social work—not hardly as glamorous, prestigious or lucrative; but she is happy.
>
> It was luck that Anne came out on top because she didn't want to go to medical school anyway.

In contrast, less than 10 percent of the boys showed any signs of wanting to avoid success. Rather, they were delighted at John's triumph and predicted a great career for him.

Generalized statements about women's ambivalence, about ambition, based on findings such as the above, become part of a myth system when they are used to make predictions and decisions about individual women. It is always necessary to allow for individual differences no matter how true the generalization. Nearly 10 percent of the boys in Horner's study *did* show a tendency to avoid success. And nearly 35 percent of the girls *did not* as the following story indicates:

> Anne is quite a lady—not only is she tops academically, but she is liked and admired by her fellow students—quite a trick in a man-dominated field. She is brilliant—but she is also a woman. She will continue to be at or near the top. And . . . always a lady.

**"Pay gap" between men and women gets wider**

| Median earnings per year (full-time workers) | | |
|---|---|---|
| | Women | Men |
| 1957 | $3,008 | $4,713 |
| 1958 | $3,102 | $4,927 |
| 1959 | $3,193 | $5,209 |
| 1960 | $3,293 | $5,417 |
| 1961 | $3,351 | $5,644 |
| 1962 | $3,446 | $5,794 |
| 1963 | $3,561 | $5,978 |
| 1964 | $3,690 | $6,195 |
| 1965 | $3,823 | $6,375 |
| 1967 | $3,973 | $6,848 |
| 1968 | $4,150 | $7,182 |
| 1969 | $4,457 | $7,664 |
| (Latest available) | | |

Source: United States Department of Commerce'

**Unemployment rate: higher for women than men**

| Rate of unemployment (average for year) | | |
|---|---|---|
| | Women | Men |
| 1960 | 5.9% | 5.4% |
| 1961 | 7.2% | 6.4% |
| 1962 | 6.2% | 5.2% |
| 1963 | 6.5% | 5.2% |
| 1964 | 6.2% | 4.6% |
| 1965 | 5.5% | 4.0% |
| 1966 | 4.9% | 3.2% |
| 1967 | 5.2% | 3.1% |
| 1968 | 4.8% | 2.9% |
| 1969 | 4.7% | 2.8% |

Source: United States Department of Labor.

**Women earn less than men in all kinds of jobs**

| Median annual earnings (full-time workers) | | |
|---|---|---|
| Occupation | Women | Men |
| Scientists | $10,000 | $13,200 |
| Professional, technical | $ 6,691 | $10,151 |
| Proprietors, managers | $ 5,635 | $10,340 |
| Clerical workers | $ 4,789 | $ 7,351 |
| Sales workers | $ 3,461 | $ 8,549 |
| Craftsmen | $ 4,625 | $ 7,978 |
| Factory workers | $ 3,991 | $ 6,738 |
| Service workers | $ 3,332 | $ 6,058 |

Source: United States Department of Labor, National Science Foundation Data for 1968.

**Most women workers are in lower-paying jobs**

| People employed as: | % of all women workers | % of all male workers |
|---|---|---|
| Proprietors managers | 4% | 14% |
| Professional technical | 15% | 14% |
| Craftsmen | 1% | 20% |
| Factory workers | 15% | 20% |
| Clerks sales workers | 42% | 13% |
| Service workers | 16% | 7% |
| Household workers | 6% | Less than 1% |

Source: United States Department of Labor.

Especially pernicious is the tendency to take a generalization beyond the level of description to make assumptions that the differences are biologically determined. This amounts to blindness to the statistical probability that most women will work for a large part of their adult lives.

## WOMEN'S IMAGE

At the present time there is an elaborate educational system designed to teach women to underestimate themselves. Society's expectations enter the teaching process before girls reach school, but once they do, school textbooks continue to keep a ceiling on the aspirations of little girls. A recent study of five social studies textbooks written for grades one to three revealed that men were shown or described in over 100 different jobs and women in less than 30. Almost all the women's jobs are those traditionally associated with women. Women are shown as having so few jobs of interest available to them that they might as well stay home and have children. But even their work at home is downplayed. Women are not shown teaching or disciplining their children, baking complicated dishes or handling money in a knowledgeable way. Because the father is making money and therefore the more important member of the family, a house is where Mr. Brown "and his family live." Even pictures show men or boys seven times as often as women or girls.

Moreover, examination of any toy catalog will show page after page of dolls and household appliances for little girls, but no little girls' outfits for engineer, chemist, lawyer or astronaut. TV commercials (bear in mind the length of time the average American child spends before the TV set) endlessly show women helpless before a pile of soiled laundry until the male voice of authority overrides hers to tell how brand X with its fast-acting enzymes will get her clothes cleaner than clean.

If a women desires or has to work, and if her early socialization hasn't "taken," then for the mature woman there are such venerable institutions as Dr. Spock to make her feel guilty for doing so, especially if she has children.

> "Why can't a woman," asked Dr. Benjamin M. Spock, "be less like a man? . . .
>
> "The absurd thing is that men go into pediatrics and obstetrics because they find them interesting and creative, and American women shun childbearing and childrearing because they don't. . . .

"Man is the fighter, the builder, the trap-maker, the one who thinks mechanically and abstractly. Woman has stayed realistic, personal, more conservative.

"Everybody can disprove me by saying these are culturally determined, but I can disprove them by saying that these are emotionally determined."

This type of rhetoric, reinforcing male vanity, has been used until recently to prevent Third World people from taking themselves seriously in occupational terms also, as the following paraphrase by Karen Oppenheim illustrates:

"Why can't a Negro," asked Dr. Benjamin M. Spock, "be less like a white? . . .

"The absurd thing is that whites go into agricultural science and overseeing because they find them interesting and creative, and American Negroes shun cotton picking and plant pruning because they don't. . . .

"Whites are the fighters, the builders, the leaders, the ones who think mechanically and abstractly. Negroes have stayed rhythmic, personal, more happy-go-lucky.

"Everybody can disprove me by saying these are culturally determined, but I can disprove them by saying that these are emotionally determined."

To the influence of textbooks, the media and books on child care we can add the fact that many young women have never had the experience of dealing with a woman in a responsible position of authority. School guidance counsellors assist in the cooling-out process by discouraging women from entering nontraditional fields of employment.

**Myth 2: If women do pursue a career they tend to be more interested in personal development than in a career as a way of life.**

Another form of this myth is "She will only get married, have children and drop out of the labor force anyway." Figures from the Women's Bureau show the fallacy in this line of reasoning. *One-tenth* of *all* women remain single, and these women work for most of their lives. In fact, those who enter the labor force by age 20 and remain unmarried will work 45 years on the average—*longer* than the 43-year average for men. In addition, *one-tenth* of all *married* women do not have children. If they enter the labor force by age 20, they will work 35 years on the average, eight years less than men. Although it is difficult to estimate the average time spent in the labor force by women with children (the tendency is to work, drop out when the children are small and then reenter), the average woman today will be in her mid-thirties by the time her youngest child is in school. If she reenters the labor force at age 35 and has no more children, she will average another 24 years of work. Women in the labor force who are widowed, separated or divorced at age 35 will work on the average another 28 years (17 percent of women in the population aged 16 or over were widowed or divorced in 1967; 15 percent of those were in the labor force).

Apart from those women who are single, widowed, divorced, married with no children or married with their youngest child in school, there are women with pre-school age children who are motivated to work either due to financial necessity or to the desire for a continuous career pattern. For all of these women it is not only (or perhaps not even primarily) their lack of motivation that prevents their career advancement so much as it is institutionalized assumptions concerning the normality of marriage, motherhood and the inevitability of withdrawal from the labor force. A striking example of this was reported by journalist Jane Harriman who wrote in a recent *Atlantic* article that she was fired from her job when she asked her boss to give her leave to have a baby. That the baby was to be illegitimate only underscores the assumptions and expectations that people have about motherhood. Why, for that matter, shouldn't there be paternity leaves, or paternity firings?

A related, equally serious, result of assuming women to be a marginal and uncommitted work force is the lack of adequate day care facilities. In 1965 the Census Bureau conducted a national study of women who had worked 27 weeks or more in 1964, either full- or part-time, and who had at least one child under 14 years of age living at home. The 6.1 million mothers surveyed had 12.3 million children under 14 years of age, of whom 3.8 million were under six years. But licensed public and private day care facilities available three years later could provide for only about half a million of those children!

The California Advisory Commission on the Status of Women, for example, had to report that the actual unmet need for children's center services was an unknown quantity. Most districts reported waiting lists from 50 to 100 percent of their present capacity. A two-year delay after being placed on a waiting list was not unusual. One out of every five poverty level residents not in the labor force, but who wanted a regular job, listed inability to obtain child care as the primary reason for not looking for work.

Even the available facilities were found to be inadequate. The problems encountered in existing programs and services included obsolete and unsafe facilities, lack of a state-level child care coordinating council, staff shortages, lack of continuity of funding, segregation of children by economic class, lack of adequate licensing standards, transportation and lack of facilities for children under two, for school-aged children up to the age of 12 years and for sick children.

**Myth 3: There will be a higher absenteeism and turnover rate amongst women than amongst men, due to the restrictions imposed by children on working mothers.**

The third myth is used to rationalize discriminatory employment practices related to women. However, in a 1969 study the Women's bureau found labor turnover rates more influenced by the skill level of the job, the age of the worker, the worker's record of job stability and the worker's length of service with the employer than by the sex of the worker. Indeed a study of occupational mobility of individuals 18 years of age and over showed that men changed occupations more frequently than women. Between January 1965 and January 1966, 10 percent of the men, as against 7 percent of the women, were employed in different occupations. Similarly, women on the average lose more workdays due to acute conditions than do men, but men lose more workdays due to chronic conditions such as heart trouble, arthritis, rheumatism and orthopedic impairment. Considering both conditions, during a one-year period, *women lost less time* than men because of illness or injury (5.3 days for women versus 5.4 days for men 17 years of age and over).

**Myth 4: Women are only working for pin money, for extras.**

The fourth myth is used to justify discrimination in employment when a job is given to a less qualified man because "she didn't need the money anyway." The Women's Bureau found 1.5 million female family heads—more than one-tenth of all families were headed by a woman in 1966—were the sole breadwinners for their families. Moreover, families headed by women were the most economically deprived: in 1967 almost one-third of such families lived in poverty, and they were the most persistently poor. Their median income was only $4,010 rising to $5,614 if the woman head was a year-round full-time worker. The income is substantially lower than the $8,168 median income of male-head families in which the male head worked full-time year-round but the wife was not in the labor force. Even where both husband and wife are working, the woman's income is often not for frivolous luxuries but means the difference between economic survival or not. In March 1967, 43 percent of those wives whose husbands' incomes were between $5,000 and $7,000 were in the labor force; 41 percent where husbands' incomes were between $3,000 and $5,000; 33 percent between $2,000 and $3,000; 27 percent between $1,000 and $2,000; and 37 percent when husbands' incomes were under $1,000.

At the state level, the California Advisory Commission on the Status of Women found nearly one in ten families in California headed by a woman. Similar to the national findings, in California economic need is the most compelling reason to work for the great majority of women with young children. The two factors most responsible for the need are the amount and the regularity of the husband's earnings. Women's earnings are not supplementary but basic to the maintenance of their family. Women comprise 35.7 percent of the California labor force, and the California economy depends significantly on women workers.

Myth 5: **Women control most of the power and wealth in American society.**

The inference that is supposed to be drawn from this notion is that women are "the power behind the throne," the major controllers of economic wealth even though they do not earn it. A weak form of the argument, for example, is that women are the major American stockholders. The argument is false. The Women's Bureau found 18 percent of the total number of shares of stock reported by public corporations were owned individually by women, 24 percent individually by men. The remaining 58 percent were held or owned by institutions, brokers and dealers. In estimated market value, stock registered in women's names was 18 percent of the total, in men's names 20 percent. A glance at the board of directors of public corporations will reveal an almost totally male membership, casting great doubt on how much social control women have, even over the stock they do own.

Women may spend a major portion of their husbands' earnings, but the expenditures are typically for the smaller consumer items. Major purchases such as those of a house or a car will be decided by the husband or by the husband and wife together, rarely by the wife alone. Most women do not even know the exact amount of their husbands' income, so it is he who has the ultimate power over how much of it she can spend. In any event, the amount of power over expenditure is nonexistent when the most important buying decision to be made is that between brand X and brand Y of detergent. Job discrimination, the inability to realize one's true potential, is a high price to pay for the dubious privilege of deciding what color socks he will wear.

**Myth 6: It will be too disruptive to an efficient work orientation if women and men are permitted to mingle on the job.**

Studies have repeatedly shown the traditional attitudes such as these are illogical, based on bias and prejudice, rather than on fact. With respect to the ego threat implied by a women co-worker or supervisor, men are likely to report that they would feel their masculinity threatened, if they do not have a working wife or if they have never worked for a female supervisor. If they have had the experience, however, their view changes to the positive. Relevant here is the fact that it is much harder for women to get the title than to get the work. Too often, women end up in clerical dead-end jobs, keep getting assigned more and more authority and responsibility as their experience and competence increase, but with no corresponding title or salary increase. They may run the office, but it will be in the old "helpmate" pattern, in the private sense of adjunct to the boss rather than in the public sense of official recognition (social or economic) from others.

The problem of women entering male fields is similar, especially if the field is one of higher status than women are usually allowed to enter. Women and men work compatibly without disruptive sexual involvement as graduate students, laboratory technicians and bank tellers. The real problem with women entering the male-dominated trades or professions, or with men entering the clerical field, would seem to be the salaries. This would create the problem of women being paid "too much" and men "too little" for what has come to be defined as appropriate for women and men.

In brief, myths concerning sexuality on the job are mostly invoked when there is a danger of a crossing-over of female and male status and pay differentials on the job. Although the principle of "equal pay for equal work" is widely accepted and sometimes even legally enforced, great care is taken to ensure that women and men are not given the same job titles and corresponding opportunities for advancement.

**Myth 7: Women are more "human-oriented," less mechanical, and they are better at tedious, boring or repetitive tasks than men are.**

The myth embodies the dual notion that women's place is in the (human-oriented) home and that women are innately inferior to men in intellectual capacity. When feminists were demanding the right to an education in the last century, educators such as Dr. Edward H. Clarke in a book entitled *Sex in Education* published in 1873, expressed learned judgments that the demand for equality in education was physically impossible. A boy could study six hours a day, according to Dr. Clarke, but if a girl spent more than four the "brain or special apparatus will suffer . . . leading to those grievous maladies which torture a woman's earthly existence, called leucorrhoea, amenorrhoea, dysmenorrhoea, chronic and acute ovaritis, prolapsus uteri, hysteria, neuralgia, and the like." While this quaint wording makes us smile at the ignorance of an earlier generation, it should be noted that Dr. Clarke was only painfully seeking a rationalization for making the value judgment that "what is" must inevitably, innately, biologically—and therefore logically—"continue to be so." Dr. Clarke was Professor of Materia Medica at Harvard from 1855 to 1872 and for five succeeding years an Overseer. He opposed the suggestion that women be admitted to Harvard College. Women were not educated equally with men; women could not be educated equally with men.

Yet few people today smile at the ignorance of today's generation in denying women equal access to a scientific education. The young woman who wants to be an engineer, astronaut, or scientist will be ridiculed out of her decision by her family, school counsellors, textbooks, and teachers, and by her peers. The woman who wants a technical education will find many colleges and trade schools do not accept women in pre-employment apprenticeship courses in fields such as carpentry and electronics. The woman who works in a factory will find herself assigned to the tedious, repetitive, boring jobs, denied on-the-job training, placed on a separate seniority list than men (last hired, last promoted, first fired) and, of course, paid less. Women are not educated equally with men; women cannot be educated equally with men. The scientific and technical arena is the last hold out of Dr. Clarke's earlier philosophy. The woman who is unable to become an engineer or a carpenter and the woman who is assigned to the tedious factory position are both being discriminated against by the same myth.

Employers still advertise in separate male and female help wanted columns; unions still advertise for journeywomen and journeymen. The journeywoman is given less training, her promotional ladder is shorter or non-existent, and she is paid less. The woman in the factory, i.e., the woman at the lowest level in the hierarchy of this form of discrimination, suffers the greatest economic deprivation. She is the least educated, most unskilled, and often her job is necessary for her sheer physical survival. Union leadership is often absent or unresponsive to her plight. If she has a family to support or is a single head of household, she does not have the time to attend union meetings that a man, because he also has a wife who is his caretaker, does. The lack of opportunity for on-the-job training and her social education to a more passive role than her male counterpart also militate against her organizing in her own self-interest as long as her wages remain at the survival level, i.e., as long as she has something—anything—to lose.

As Marjorie B. Turner points out, we know nothing about the comparative propensity of women and men to join unions on an industry-wide basis. The Women's Bureau reports that 1 out of 7 women in the nation's labor force, but 1 out of 4 men workers, belonged to a union in 1966. Whether it is a reflection of sex labeling in jobs, discrimination, segregated locals, or difficulty or disinterest in organizing women is unknown.

The evidence regarding innate sex differences in mechanical and verbal aptitudes is sufficiently contradictory that no generalizations are warranted. Through the preschool and early school years, girls exceed boys in both verbal performance and ability with numbers. By high school, boys fairly consistently excel at mathematics. In addition, boys more accurately assess their abilities and performance by high school, whereas girls seem to show an earlier decline in tested performance. Such differences could, of course, be genetic. However, it seems equally or more plausible to suggest that they are related to social pressures operating differently on women and men to mold them into the adult roles they are assigned by tradition to play. As children, girls are taught to be passive and submissive, and this is conducive to grade school performance. By high school, boys are taught to prepare for careers, and this is conducive to high school performance. The cultural interpretation is consistent with Matina Horner's findings regarding the stronger motive to avoid success in college women than in college men. Until a culture evolves in which both sexes are treated as *people* with equal opportunities and expectations, the questions of genetic differences in intellectual functioning will have to remain moot.

Even granting that sex differences may have a genetic base, the statistical picture that emerges is still one of highly overlapping curves for women and men, rather than separate ones. We would be led to predict perhaps a 60:40 or smaller split in the sexes among certain occupations, but not one that is 100:0. Clearly, whether or not sex differences in mechanical aptitude are genetically determined, the current labor market certainly assumes that they are. But evidence to support the opposite conclusion was provided by the demonstrated competence of women in a wide range of occupations during World Wars I and II. Even today, the Women's Bureau reports that by mid-1968 women were being or had been trained as apprentices in 47 skilled occupations. Many of the apprenticeships, such as that of cosmetologist or dressmaker, reflected traditional roles. But some women were being trained as clock and watch repairman, electronic technician, engraver, optical mechanic, precision lens grinder, machinist, plumber, draftsman, electrical equipment repairer, electronic subassembly repairer and compositor.

Women's entry into traditionally male apprenticeship fields illustrates the fallacy of the myth that women are better than men at tedious, boring or repetitive tasks. It is doubtful whether the boredom, repetitiveness or tediousness differs greatly between a clock and watch repairman (male) and a typist (female) or between a precision lens grinder (male) and a dental technician (female). As Caroline Bird has documented, women's work in one part of the world or at one historical period may be man's work in another part of the world or at another time. What doesn't change is that whatever men do is regarded as more important, and gets more rewards, than what women do. The boundaries are defined by status, not aptitude, for even in traditionally female fields the persons in the highest positions of authority are most likely to be male.

### Myth 8: Women need to be "protected" because of their smaller size.

There is no question but that women are physically smaller on the average than are men, but the inferences drawn from, and the restrictions imposed by, the biological fact are socially determined. In other cultures and at other times it has been women who have pulled the plows or carried burdens on their heads because of their presumed superior physical strength. Today it is men who suffer from hernias, back troubles and a shorter life expectancy because of the heavier physical tasks they are expected to assume. The industrial revolution made most, if not all, heavy physical work unnecessary, providing employers are willing to invest in the necessary laborsaving equipment. As long as there is a marginal, exploitable, male labor force (as has been the case with Third World peoples in America), it is often cheaper for the employer to use manual labor than to provide the requisite equipment.

Protective laws with respect to lifting should be extended to cover all *people* not restricted to one sex. Where lifting is required, a person's physical ability to hold the job should be medically, not sexually, determined. There may be some jobs involving lifting which only a few women—or men—would be able to perform. At the present time, there seems little inclination for women to enter such fields as professional football. (There is one exception, and she may truly prove the rule; she was squashed by an opposing guard.) There has, however, been much resistance to women jockeys, whose smaller size is a decided asset.

As long as there are protective laws governing women only, and not protective laws for workers in general, such laws can be used to perpetuate discrimination. A job requiring heavy lifting can be placed in the lower rung of a promotional hierarchy, even if experience at that job bears no relation to subsequent positions in the hierarchy. It has the effect of preventing women from entering *any* of the positions in the hierarchy because they are not allowed to enter the one with the weight-lifting restriction at the bottom.

With respect to restrictions on night work ostensibly concerning the safety of women going to and from their jobs, the rationalization only seems to occur when the overtime or shift work involved would place her in a higher status occupational category as well. As baby-sitter, as char-woman, as librarian, as telephone operator, as nurse, as keypuncher, the woman working at night is considered perfectly capable of looking after her own safety. It is well worth remembering that men often place women on pedestals only so they do not have to look us in the eye!

## VICIOUS CIRCLE

The myth systems that perpetuate sexual discrimination bring us round full circle. Women are stereotyped as lacking in aggressive and managerial qualities; if they do have the qualities or the opportunity to learn them, laws and customs are invoked to prevent their being used. Women and men are not judged as individuals based on demonstrated competence, but on the basis of sexual stereotypes. Moreover, women's underestimation of their own abilities combines with others' underestimation of their abilities to produce the declining status of women in today's labor force.

As Cynthia Fuchs Epstein points out, success is difficult for women because of the nature of informal channels of support and communication. Breaking a color, ethnic or sex occupational barrier means that the newcomers have not shared the same worlds as their colleagues. Casual chats, informal rituals, jokes, shared experiences—all become strained and serve to keep the newcomer in the psychological position of "the stranger."

It is true that women are becoming more emancipated, but it is an emancipation from the home and not towards higher status in the labor force. Although the mass media provide great fanfare for women as they become "firsts" in traditionally male fields, the publicity obscures the overall decline in women's status in the labor force. The Horatio Alger myth of American society was always a cruel hoax. Perpetuated with respect to women, it is simply laughable, when the average woman with five years of college can expect to earn the equivalent of a man with a high school education.

## SUGGESTED READINGS

Shulamith Firestone, *The Dialectic of Sex*. New York: Morrow, 1970. A radical critique of society explaining why feminists cannot expect to accomplish change on the basis of equality in the labor market alone.

Juanita Kreps, *Sex in the Marketplace: American Women at Work.* Baltimore, Md.: Johns Hopkins Press, 1971. Women are overeducated for the jobs they hold, and Kreps considers why.

Robert W. Smuts, *Women and Work in America.* New York: Schocken, 1971. A lucid historical review of women and occupations from 1890 to 1950 that illuminates reasons for the current occupational division of labor.

# Toward a Society of Neuters

**Charles Winick**

Charles Winick's analysis of the desexualization of American life is probably unknown to most feminist sympathizers, yet his thesis is highly charged. He dissects the more mundane elements of our society, such as television, popular music, dress, the arts, and in the selection here, sports, to highlight the breakdown of sex-based differences. Deploring this trend, he uses labels such as "the way of the Neuter" or "the country of the bland" to describe this process and its consequences.

Is Winick being sexist? Does he have a romantic desire to return to the days when males were virile gentlemen and females had the vapors? Not overtly, for his argument is that a total breakdown of the recognized differences between male and female may destroy the basis of their attraction for each other, hence threaten the very survival of the species. That is what he says, yet his analysis of sports hints at a regret that women are beginning to look and perform like men. Nevertheless, Winick's data on how women suddenly and rapidly are meeting male physical performance records implicitly substantiate the feminist thesis that "inferior" performance by females is a reflection of societal expectations rather than a sign of genuine weakness.

Some may discount studies such as Winick's on the ground that a breakdown in sex differences on this level is trivial, because

---

women still lack power, prestige, and money—the keystone trinity of our society. Are these minor accommodations merely a device used to mollify women? Or are they precursors of deeper changes in the fabric of society—having been instituted first because they were the simplest? What evidence would you need to support or repudiate these opposing theories?

---

Archeologists are fond of saying that were it not for graves and garbage piles, buried under the ruins of successive societies, we might know relatively little about the character and lives of people in the past. Today, in our economy of abundance and condition of perpetual war, the litter of civilization seems to be more than sufficient for archeologists in years to come. We have produced enough garbage; it has even been transmuted into art and political rhetoric. Yet it is doubtful that the leftovers of our lives will tell enough. If we succeed in completing the nihilistic formula for self-destruction that has made it possible for the nightmares of Leonardo and St. John to come true, the radioactive garbage will be too hot to handle and the graves will be made of whole continents.

After World War II, the tide of human consciousness and its social expression began to move in a radically different direction in the United States. As a new generation grew up in the midst of this transformation, it was difficult for their parents to appreciate either the meaning or magnitude of the change. While we continued to display the relics of western tradition, we largely ignored the arrival of the New People, the troops of an invading army. Their advent went virtually unnoticed and they quietly took over while we were out fighting the cold war.

They set up camps and fought the battle of the cool war, which led to substantial changes in personality and social life. Many of the changes are not reflected in the palpable material objects of our society that would primarily concern the archeologist. The troop movements slipped by with the invisibility of gradual social change, under the cover of darkness which clouded what was to be later seen as a massive shift of human consciousness and its social expression.

Social change is almost invisible to those inside it. But the cumulative impact of the transformation of our lives is all too apparent in the 1960's. The New People have taken over; they are the authorities when it comes to setting the tone of our living together. When we recognize them at all, it is as figures from some elaborate entertainment which has little to do with sensible, everyday life. We hardly notice the invasion because it has been so widespread and successful.

Our infinitely manipulatable, no-deposit, no-return world reflects the compact which man has made with machines, particularly the machinery of his own destruction. It is such a truism, so much an everyday fact of life, that we have almost become comfortable in our plastic wilderness. The New People dress in clothes that make the Martians and the Space Maiden look conservative. They accept and participate in the destruction of obsolete concepts of identity, sexuality, and ways of living. We have failed to recognize them; they are, in fact, invisible. They are ourselves.

Archeologists of the future may regard a radical dislocation of sexual identity as the single most important event of our time. Ethology, the science concerned with animal behavior and interaction with environment, has repeatedly hinted in recent years that radical changes in sex roles may lead to extermination of whole species. This does not mean that we, the New People, will fail to survive or that we are unable to create a viable substitute for rejected lifestyles. It does suggest that the new tone of life, a bitter, metallic existence, may simply not be worth the price of enduring it.

The change could be related to our downgrading of two radical but unrelated developments which entered the western world at about the same time: gunpowder and romantic love. Gunpowder was introduced to the west during the late medieval period, just about when the troubadours were creating what we have since come to know as romantic love, with its lack of fulfillment and idealization of the beloved beyond mere sensual love. The atom bomb has made gunpowder less significant, and many forces, in our day of disposable sex, make romantic love a less meaningful ideal. The bomb is a model of the new technology that is profoundly affecting every aspect of social and sex roles. The decline of romantic love reflects and reinforces other changes that are modifying expressions of the most basic difference in any society—the difference between its men and women.

The hostess at a dinner party attended by Albert Einstein, according to one of the many charming stories told about him, observed the scientist walking on her terrace and looking at the stars. She identified herself as an amateur astronomer and pointed upward: "Every night I come out here and study Venus with my telescope." Einstein followed her suggestion to look through the telescope and said, "Your hobby is very interesting. But, I believe, that planet is Jupiter." The woman was very impressed: "You certainly are brilliant to be able to tell the sex of a planet at such a great distance." It is increasingly difficult to tell the sex of many things, at almost any distance, in America today. As masculinity and femininity show less polarization and fewer differences, extremes of other kinds are beoming blurred into a neuter. This modification of the American way of life could be the most significant change of our time and be intimately related to our society's ability to survive. . . .

## FUN AND GAMES

When *The Father* is placed in a straitjacket by his wife near the climax of Strindberg's play, he shouts: "Omphale, Omphale!" referring to the Queen of Lydia who employed Hercules as a servant, wore the great athlete's lion-skin, and hunted with his club and spear. Today's American women are emulating Omphale although not too long ago embroidery and painting china were almost their only approved leisure pursuits.

Throughout most of the nineteenth century, our prudery and assumption of women's delicacy had made it almost impossible for men and women to participate in outdoor activities together. In the late 1870's, croquet became the first outdoor game in which both sexes could join. Not until the liberalization of bathing costumes during the 1920's was there any substantial acceptance of women's right to enjoy recreation in free association with men and costumed in accordance with the situation.

*Annie, Get Your Gun* was an extraordinary example of art's ability to predict life. So many women followed Annie's advice that they now account for 32 percent of our 25,000,000 gun owners. Along with the gun, they took over as town marshal. A generation after Irving Berlin's prophetic words, the wife was most often the person who made key family decisions.[1] Such leadership is only one reflection of her recent dominance of other facets of leisure.

The new look in the sporting life was signaled in 1964 by appointment of a woman to announce the Kansas City Athletics' games on television. Although the best man competitor can usually beat the best woman in a sport, there has been a strong improvement in the quantity and quality of women's participation in athletics and competitive sports. In the defiantly masculine arena, women's new role is certainly a sign that they now share some of the competitiveness that had long been regarded as a male trait.

Although women have the advantage of a more compact frame than do men, menstrual periods interfere with their training. Nonetheless, their athletic performance has been improving continually, as they become heavier and taller. The average American women is fourteen pounds heavier than her counterpart of thirty years ago and the typical Miss America contestant who stood five feet high in 1921 was six inches taller by 1962.[2]

In only two generations, the average woman's foot has jumped from 6 to 8, and sample shoe sizes have increased from 4-4½ to 5½-6. Feet have become so much wider that only B and C widths of many popular lines are in stock. A and AA narrow widths, regularly available as recently as the 1950's can be bought only on special order and AAA is carried by very few shops.[3]

Women's shoulders are becoming broader in relation to their hips and their physique is otherwise assuming more masculine proportions. Today's women are also more muscular and mesomorphic than their ancestors and mesomorphy is positively correlated with strength and power.[4] Such changes contribute to the decrease in sexual dimorphism and are occurring even though the decreasing age at menarche provides less time for growth to occur.

Form follows function and the women in earlier societies in which they had dominant roles, like the Germans described by Tacitus or the Congo Andombis, were also characterized by physiques with traditional masculine characteristics. In societies where women take initiative in work and wooing, like the Bosjemans, they are often taller than men.

As American women become increasingly mesomorphic, their personalities could well become more aggressive, self-starting, and dominant than their mothers' or grandmothers'. Such changes in temperament and character and more accepting social attitudes on the part of the community have facilitated women's participation in sports. Although women who seriously engaged in sports a generatio ago were rare, many now regularly compete in squash, handball, and other formerly male sports.

Women contenders use sophisticated training procedures and set goals that are progressively more difficult. Wilma Rudolph's preparation for the 1960 Olympic track competition was typical of the thoroughness that has enabled many women to break records more spectacularly than their men counterparts. Another reason could be that men have been competing for so long that they have already approached their potential. Even in medium-

and long-distance swimming, where so much depends on the body's upper musculature, women's systematic clipping of Amateur Athletic Union records is superior to men's. By 1962, women had shaved 81.4 seconds from the 1946 400-meter freestyle time of 5′26.7″; men cut only 37.6 seconds from their 1946 time of 4′49.8″. Women pruned 3′22.1″ from the 1,500-meter freestyle time of 22′8.1″ between 1946 and 1962; men nicked a mere 2′7.4″ from their mark of 19′23.1″.

Our country's swimmers and divers won an unprecedented seven of ten women's events in the 1964 Olympics, and in 1960 Miss Rudolph proved the efficacy of her training by becoming the first American woman to win three Olympic track and field gold medals. The United States' women's showing in their 1964 Los Angeles meet with Russia was especially impressive because of the Russian advantage in size and musculature.

Women are not only competing more actively on the playing field but can increasingly be found in the audiences for baseball, horse racing, and boxing. The sport least comfortable for a spectator is professional football, often played in weather cold enough to require fur coats and mufflers, but women now represent two-fifths of its audience, while more and more men watch football on television. Of the women expressing a preference for attending outdoor events, 42 percent actually attend them as often as they would like, compared with only 33 percent of the men.[5] Women who attend sports events are hardly passive spectators and can ventilate aggression when they boo, cheer, heckle, hiss, jeer, scream, shout, and taunt for victory.[6] It is not surprising that female sports fans are giving less and less time to reports of sewing circles and knitting or flower clubs and teas in women's pages of newspapers. Sixty-nine percent of American women who look at newspapers open them to the sports pages, where they read about competitors who beat, blast, bomb, boff, bury, clout, flay, paste, jolt, rip, scalp, sink, slug, swamp, tear, trim, and whip one another.[7]

Today's prime suburban blood vendetta may be taking place on tennis courts. Only 30 percent of the 4,100,000 tennis players were women in 1946 but they now account for 45 percent of our 8,500,000 players. Women's tennis has changed from exercise to competition, with tournaments at every age level. Women have become more active in tournament, public court, and club play at the very time that tennis has involved more speed and power. A powerful serve tends to be followed by a rush to the net, putting away an opponent's return before it bounces.

Women adapt to the new game in a variety of ways. Althea Gibson developed a very powerful flat serve with a whipping wrist motion that was very difficult to return. Billie Jean King is preeminent in women's tennis today because of her aggressiveness around the court, rushing net game, and strong ground strokes. Others skillfully serve to corners of the service box so that an opponent must race off the court in order to return the ball. Some serve with slices and twists in which the ball is hit at an angle and bounces high and away. Others who concentrate on their backcourt game emulate William Tilden, perhaps the greatest tennis player of all time.

Paddle tennis is one of the few sports in which a woman can do about as well as a man. The game is faster and wilder than tennis and is played with a hard rubber ball on a raised wooden platform that is about half the length and width of a regulation tennis court, sanded and surrounded by a wire fence. Its near-domination by women may be one reason that paddle tennis is an important "social" game.

Women have also taken over the golf course, that traditional male Garden of Eden. They represented ten percent of our 2,450,000 golfers in 1946, but now account for over one-third of the 7,750,000 Americans who tee off regularly. In July 1965, the U.S. Women's Open became the first such event to get network television coverage. Any lack of strength that limits the length of women's wood shots can be largely overcome by their superior manual dexterity and deftness in medium- and even long-iron play. A three-inch putt and a three-hundred-yard drive, after all, each count for one stroke. Women who concentrate on an accurate short game and perfect their chipping and putting can apply their accuracy to best advantage.

Women's great success in tournament golf has demonstrated that power and strength can be less important than grace and rhythm, especially within one hundred twenty-five yards of the cup. Gary Player, who is only 5′7″, stands up against much bigger men. Chichi Rodriguez is 5′6″ and weighs 126 pounds, but can drive a ball as far as Arnold Palmer.

The first woman to get an athletic scholarship at the University of Kentucky received it for golf prowess. Women now play on other varsity teams, so that a coed may play against a male. A woman has been a member of Stetson University's varsity tennis team and Pam Hayes and Martha Leveritt swam well enough to make the men's squad at Tulane. Women college athletes have so far been confined to golf, tennis, and swimming, but baseball and basketball are obviously next.[8]

Even sports that were once regarded as hazardous seem to hold no terror for many women. In sledding and tobogganning, their participation averages 1.38 times per year in contrast to 2.2 for men. Women represent a growing proportion of the 3,500,000 American skiers, whose number is increasing at the rate of 20 percent each year as the sport becomes an occasion for social activity that cuts across class lines. Any fear of disfigurement that once deterred many women skiers is no longer operative.[9]

Free fall parachuting was formerly considered so risky that only men attempted it less than a decade ago, but the 20,000 women recreational sky jumpers now represent one-fifth of the total. Surfing was also once too dangerous for women, but they now account for one-third of all surfers. Water skiing has more women than men devotees, and all-girl rowing teams compete successfully with men.

The male sanctuary in the wilderness has yielded to women, who have been heeding the call of the wild in such numbers that they now do more camping than men. The fair sex also represents an increasing proportion of our 42 million boaters although not too long ago the sport was a symbol of man's untrammeled spirit and proud seafaring heritage. Joshua Slocum's bringing the thirty-seven foot *Spray* into the harbor of Newport, R. I., on June 27, 1898, marked the first time a man had sailed around the world by himself.[10] The seagoing Thoreauism represented by Captain Slocum has become a historical memory as women have bent the rigging of men's traditional nautical fantasies into new shapes. Frank Lloyd Wright's comment that he needed the customer's wife as an ally has not been lost on builders of yachts and cabin cruisers. Interior designer Doris Slane, who works exclusively with ship interiors, has asked, "If a man gets what he wants in a hull, why should a wife be stuck in a little old dark galley?"[11] In deference to their new first mate, many vessels now have electric kitchens, and exteriors that were traditionally white or mahogany come in pastels. Bunk and cockpit cushions, countertops, cabin curtains, and even the spinnaker appear in decorator colors.

Another outdoor activity that has attracted many women is horseback riding, and girls and young women now engage in more horseback riding than boys and young men. Seventy percent of the riders under 21 are female and women in the northeast ride four times as frequently as men. A former president of the United States Pony Clubs gave some reasons: "Girls have the temperament to be patient and persistent. Boys . . . don't like a sport in which girls can compete on an equal basis with them."[12] Women used to wear skirts when they rode side-saddle but changed to divided skirts, culottes, breeches under skirts, and most recently, men's riding breeches, once they sat astride the horse. Women's new participation in riding is important now that horsemanship has become a middleclass sport and more people ride saddle horses than did before the automobile. Women have also become much more active in showing, jumping, and riding at horse shows. Women outnumber men on the United States' show jumping team, which swept the 1967 European shows.

Participation by women has changed other sports and games. Twenty-five years ago, the tennis racket was unpainted and had a simple wood grip but today it is painted, varnished, multicolored, has a leather grip, and could decorate a boudoir wall. The throat connecting head with shaft is tapered, where it was once straight, and the head has become more shapely. Perhaps the most revolutionary development in tennis equipment during the last half century is the steel racket, which was used by all three American quarter-finalists in the 1967 National Singles Championship. Two slender tubes connect the handle to the head's graceful curve and contribute to the racket's delicate light appearance.

Lack of color once characterized the gut used in high-priced rackets as well as the silk in less expensive models. Today's best gut is likely to be light blue with royal blue striping, and nylon stringing comes in stripes and white, brown, and blue. Racket covers, once black or green, are available in a wide range of colors. The brown or black saxophone-shaped container for tennis gear that was used by many players is being replaced by brightly colored soft plastic cases. Even the gray or black cement or asphalt tennis court is metamorphosing to red or green concrete or composition.

At the same time that women have helped to soften the starkness of tennis courts and equipment, their costumes have become less feminine. The long tennis dress has yielded to the straight shift line and to white shorts and shirts. Husband and wife wear a similar shirt, often the Perry with a tiny green wreath applique, or the Lacoste, with a small green alligator applique. Both sexes sport identical white sneakers and socks and are likely to wear a similar white cable stitch pullover or cardigan for going to and from the court and warming up. From the late 1940's into the early 1950's, some women followed the lead of Gussie Moran and wore tennis clothes with feminine necks and pleated ruffles. But the sugar-plum-fairy look is as obsolete as a wire-strung racket, Miss Moran's lace-ruffled bloomers have left the courts, and the functional simple look is the overhead smash of the season.[13]

Women are largely responsible for the move away from relatively informal skiing costumes to colors like pink and burgundy for each part of the day, and even skiing techniques show a distaff influence. They began to change after one of the few scientific analyses ever made of a sport's established techniques. For decades, students were taught to make turns by the rotation method, in which shoulders move in the direction of a turn. In the early 1950's, Professor Stefan Kruckenhauser of the Austrian State Ski School analyzed motion pictures of famous races and concluded that champion skiers turned their shoulders in a direction away from the turn.[14] He developed the reverse shoulder method of turning, moving shoulders away from the turn. Experience with the reverse shoulder method eventually gave rise to another innovation in Wedeln, which means to wag, like a dog's tail. This sharp s-turn is a change in direction by swaying the hips from side to side in a rhumba-like motion. Wedeln is more elegant and fluid than longer and more traditional turns like a Stem Christie or Christiana. Some of the American enthusiasm for Wedeln, and its quicker and more graceful version called the Mambo, results from women's realization of the high octane potential of graceful hip movements while going down a ski slope in colorful skin-tight ski pants or jump suits. As the manager of a Grosse Pointe ski shop noted, "A good fit is when you can tell if a coin in the gal's back pocket is heads or tails."[15]

American women's extensive participation has substantially changed the automobile rallye, in which a distance is covered at a prescribed average speed per hour on each section of the course. Participants lose points by going either too fast or too slow, for damages to the car, getting lost, or not having route cards stamped at various checkpoints.

A typical European rallye team consists of two men, but many American rallye teams consist of a man driver and a woman as navigator or co-driver. In Europe, the prescribed rate is difficult to maintain because the course often includes badly rutted or damaged roads, often flooded or covered by ice or snow. Drivers on the 2,712 icy miles of the Monte Carlo rallye pack axes, shovels, and chains. Paddy Hopkirk, the 1964 winner, described the course "It was marvelous . . . intolerable conditions all the way . . . let's hope next year the weather is worse."

Largely as a result of women's participation, the competition in American rallyes is less grueling and tends to be based on precision rather than speed, endurance, and courage. The course seldom contains roads that are badly damaged or include unexpected hazards. Women navigators often work the computers that determine the accuracy with which speed is being maintained and that were developed because a slide rule was not precise enough.

European rallyes still retain the competition's original character as a test of an automobile's stamina under difficult conditions of everyday use. In the 1965 Monte Carlo competition, only thirty-five of two hundred thirty-seven starters reached the goal within prescribed time limits and the winning car required eight changes of tires to complete the last 378 miles. A car that wins such a rallye uses its victory to convince potential purchasers that it can cope with difficult driving conditions. In America, precision is so important that a manufacturer seldom uses a rallye victory as a significant sales point.

Many American rallye drivers wear straight line suits, ties, and snappy little caps. Dandification has become so important that designer John Weitz has written a book of advice on clothing to wear in different racing situations. "A race driver's clothes. . . can give him confidence . . . full of dash and daring and personal display . . . be sure *not* to wear the scarf Ascot fashion . . . ."[16] In contrast, European drivers are far more likely to wear sweaters or work clothes.

Not unexpectedly, indoor recreational activities reflect much distaff influence. Time was, men would plan an evening with their chums to go bowling. They are less likely to do so without wives or girl friends now that so many of our 25 million bowlers are women. Many bowl while using closed-circuit television to watch their children playing in an adjacent nursery. Soft pastel colors prettify many a bowling alley and balls and carrying cases come in royal blue, Kelly green, and red. A "gutter" is now a "channel."

Women's interest in billiards has enabled the sport to gain new adherents almost as spectacularly as it had previously lost them during the Depression, during the course of which the 40,000 "pool halls" declined by 80 percent. The "pool parlor" has evolved from dinginess and spittoons into the family "billiard center" that services 14 million Americans. Many "centers" have thick carpeting and tables covered in tangerine, rust, coral, and pale blue rather than traditional green. The bright and airy rooms are lavishly appointed and usually have automatic scorekeepers and fluorescent lighting.

A 1961 photograph of Queen Mother Elizabeth lining up a shot helped greatly in making billiards more socially acceptable.

Masako Katsura, the first woman to try for the world's three-cushion billiard title, suggested another reason for billiards' appeal: "It is just the right kind of sport for women. You use every part of the body, all the muscles, and it keeps the body beautiful."[17] But a Brooklyn man who is less sympathetic to women's needs complained: "The pool parlor was the only place a fellow could go to relax and get away from women. Now even this refuge is gone. The only place left is the men's room."[18]

Ever since commercial billiard lounges came from behind the eight-ball in 1962, sales of home equipment have increased and more than a quarter-million home tables are sold in a typical year. Most tables are used by the whole family and many come in round or elliptoid shapes that blend with unusually shaped rooms and can be transformed into surfaces for dining or ping pong.

As green billiard tables have been giving way to decorator colors, the proportion of women to men gambling at the green felt crap tables of Las Vegas has doubled over the last ten years. Dice traditionally requires its participants to be aggressive masters of their fate. The dice are thrown forward vigorously and the game's vocabulary is challenging, masculine, profane, and sexualized ("come to me, baby").

Women's increased interest in shooting craps may have a reciprocal relationship to men's growing participation in Las Vegas roulette over the last decade. Roulette has long been regarded as a feminine game because a bettor passively waits for the ball to come to rest in a slot after someone else has spun the wheel. Gambling is thus reflecting crisscrossing of sex roles, if the 12 million visitors who throw three billion dollars across the Las Vegas gambling tables in a year are typical.

One of the few leisure activities resisting ambisexuality is chess, with men representing approximately 99 percent of America's 35 million chess players. One reason could be the game's symbolic attack on the father-king. Men chess players seem to have a combativeness that is less likely to be found in women and even an outstanding woman player like Lisa Lane is no match for a male master.

Poker still remains the most popular man's card game. A poker game is often played in an anti-feminine atmosphere, with queens referred to as "whores."[19] Fumes from cigars, cigarettes, and the passing of wind seem to be an acceptable part of the game's anal and scatological framework. The stag atmosphere is brilliantly evoked in the opening scene of *The Odd Couple*, in which participants in a weekly poker game loosen their ties, remove their jackets, curse, spill their drinks and cigarette butts on the floor, and otherwise behave in a manner that would not gladden their wives.

## FOOTNOTES AND REFERENCES

1. Walter Carlson, "Woman's Pocketbook Domain," *New York Times,* August 8, 1965, p. F12.

2. Professor Martin Samit has been most helpful in the preparation of this section.

3. For example, Bloomingdale's in New York used to carry AA widths in regular stock in its Briolett line but now only gets them on special order basis.

4. Joyce A. Perbix, "Relationship Between Somatotype and Motor Fitness in Women," *Research Quarterly of the American Association for Health and Physical Education,* 25, 1954, pp. 84-90.

5. *National Recreation Survey:* A Report to the Outdoor Recreation Resources Review Committee, ORRRC Study Report, 19. Washington: Government Printing Office, 1962. Other figures on outdoor recreational activity cited in the chapter derive from this report.

6. John Del Torto, "On Gambling," *Neurotica,* No. 6, 1950, pp. 11-22.

7. Bureau of Advertising, *A Study of the Opportunity for Exposure to National Newspaper Advertising.* New York: The Bureau , 1965, p. 9.

8. Sid Ross and Neal Ashby, "Rah, Rah, Girls, Fight! Fight! Fight!", *Parade,* February 23, 1964, pp. 6-7.

9. James A. Knight, "Motivation in Skiing," *Western Journal of Surgery, Obstetrics, and Gynecology,* 69, 1961, pp. 395-398.

10. Joshua Slocum, *Sailing Alone Around the World.* New York: Sheridan House, 1954.

11. "Mates Outrank Skippers on Deep Mauve Seas," *New York Times,* January 19, 1964, p. 8.

12. "Horsemanship Becomes a Middle-Class Sport," *New York Times,* October 25, 1965, p. 44.

13. "What's New at the Net?" *New York Herald Tribune,* June 12, 1964, p. 14.

14. Austrian Association of Professional Ski Teachers, *The New Official Austrian Ski System.* New York: A. S. Barnes, 1958.

15. *Time,* January 6, 1967, p. 62.

16. John Weitz, *Sports Clothes for Your Sports Car.* New York: Sports Car Press, 1958.

17. J. Campbell Bruch, "Queen of Cues," *New York Times Magazine,* March 23, 1952, pp. 38-39.

18. "The Inquiring Photographer," *New York Daily News,* February 8, 1964, p. 15.

19. Ralph R. Greenson, "On Gambling" *American Imago,* 4, 1947, pp. 61-77. See *America's No. 1 Participant Sport* (Association of Playing Card Manufacturers, New York: 1960) for details of card game preferences by sex.

## SUGGESTED READINGS

Karl Bedarnik, *The Male in Crisis,* New York: Knopf, 1970. In contradiction to Sexton or Winick, Bedarnik argues that the "feminization" of the male is necessary for human survival.

Evelyne Sullerot, *Women, Society, and Change.* New York: McGraw-Hill, 1971. Data from many countries about the role of women in some areas—education, politics, work, family—suggest that unisex is not so near as Winick fears.

# Adjusting the Lives of Women to the Establishment

Jessie Bernard

Jessie Bernard analyzes the life styles of women who, via their professional careers, have broken the discriminatory patterns, at least on the surface. Her discussion illustrates the direction current social science research is taking in an effort to unravel the complexity of sexism as a process. Any woman working for a career will find sooner or later that she has to make decisions about family and career—or family vs. career. What young woman working for a Ph.D. thinks of university nepotism rules that may short-circuit her career if she marries a fellow student? Today's young woman may be able to combine career and marriage, in part precisely because of the research that Bernard makes public, but most of the women Bernard reports on were unlikely to have had this opportunity. This is one reason why feminists encourage research of this kind—because it exposes patterns of closed opportunities that are not apparent to the women who are making choices.

In a counterpoint to Suelzle's article, Bernard recognizes that her very mode of analysis might be sexist, for it presupposes the value of a full-time career. Her final paragraphs hint that women's liberation—the elimination of sexism—may mean men's liberation and benefit society as a whole. This seems to contradict Winick.

---

Are the two viewpoints necessarily incompatible? Can science provide the final answers?

Bernard's paper also reminds us that the "females" and "males" discussed throughout this book are not two-dimensional statistics. They are persons who feel, plan, and act. They make deep commitments to others, forming ties that at times complicate their own self-fulfillment. Literature has traditionally been one source for guidance on the meaning of social events for individual persons. How could a social scientist be more humanistic? What data could she or he turn to?

---

## CAREER PATTERNING

The discussion of role patterns so far has been fairly general. That is, it applies to women of all occupational levels. All have to struggle to find ways to reconcile their several functions. But for women at the highest levels, in the technical, scientific, and professional occupations, there are unique and peculiar additional problems. Not only do they, like other working mothers, have to find ways to provide for child care, but also, like their male confreres, they have the by-no-means ignorable problem of acquiring difficult professional skills and competencies before they enter their work roles and of maintaining them during interruptions, if any, in their work—or career—histories.

Thinking and policy have therefore taken quite different tacks in dealing with women in the several work-history patterns. For those in the lowest levels, on assistance rolls, policy has been designed to encourage—*coerce* would not be too strong a term—a two-role pattern. For women in the middle occupation and income brackets, who worked, when they did, because they enjoyed working or wanted to increase family income, there has been, despite recommendations by one commission after another, little positive encouragement in the form of help, either by government or by industry, especially in the form of child-care assistance, but neither has there been, as in the era of the one-role ideology, positive and active discouragement. But for women in the highest levels to whom the term *career women* is sometimes pejoratively applied there has been, if anything, active discouragement, even in some cases hostility. The career woman is required to order her life in complete conformity to the demands of her profession and to pay whatever price is exacted for deviation from them. Some of the possible ways of doing this are summarized here.

There are four variables whose timing, at least theoretically, allows them to be partially controlled by professional women in planning how to accommodate their child-bearing and child-rearing functions to the demands of their careers: (1) age at marriage, (2) age at childbearing, (3) age at professional preparation, and (4) age of assumption or resumption of professional practice. These are certainly not independent variables; each depends on the others. The first will, of course, usually precede the second; and the third, the fourth.

It might well be argued that women actually do not have partial control over these variables. The pressure on them to marry, as just noted, is so great that they feel they must marry fairly young, for if they wait all the desirable men will be committed. They have a valid point there, too, for the optimum age at marriage, as judged in terms of stability under present circumstances, is 22 for women and 24 for men. With so much pressure put on them to marry ("Better dead than unwed") it is doubtful if there really is much choice involved. But at least theoretically some control is possible. The age at which they bear children is also only partially under control despite the increasing dependability of contraception. And the age at which professional preparation is undertaken may depend on a variety of factors, including availability of support and access to facilities.

Granting that there are practical forces limiting any young woman's choices, we can still examine some of the possibilities for different patternings. In general, eight kinds of patterns, subsumed under three general categories—early interrupted, late interrupted, and uninterrupted—are possible as shown. The numbers refer to the four major contingencies in the careers of women, namely (1) marriage, (2) childbearing, (3) professional preparation, and (4) assumption or resumption of professional practice.

Eight career patterns

| | | | | | | |
|---|---|---|---|---|---|---|
| A. | 3 | 1 | 2 | 4 | | Early-interrupted pattern |
| B. | 3 | 4 | 1 | 2 | 4 | Late-interrupted pattern |
| C. | 3 | 1 | 4 | 2 | 4 | " " " |
| D. | 1 | 3 | 4 | 2 | 4 | " " " |
| E. | 1 | 3 | 2 | 4 | | " " " |
| F. | 1 | 2 | 3 | 4 | | Uninterrupted pattern |
| G. | 1 | – | 3 | 4 | | " " " |
| H. | – | – | 3 | 4 | | " " " |

The length of the interruptions is, of course, itself a variable. It might be as brief as a short maternity leave or as long as the time it takes for a last child to reach college, the future seeming to tend more toward the first option than the second. Garfinkle (1969) reports "the rather astonishing change which is taking place in the work lives of women, namely that the effects of the birth of a child on work life continuity is rapidly diminishing" (p. 5). He reports many cases in which women work almost to the time of delivery "and then returning to work after a time lapse hardly longer than a somewhat lengthy vacation or the time their husband might require to recover from a fairly minor illness" (p. 5). The crucial component is the timing of the break between *3* and *4* and its length.

### The early-interrupted pattern

It has become customary to derive an overall picture of "the average woman" in terms of an early-interrupted work history: labor-force participation until the birth of the first child, return when the last child is in school or soon thereafter.

Among talented women, Ginzberg's study showed about one-fourth in some form of interrupted pattern. Freedman reported an early-interrupted pattern as preferred among Vassar seniors (Freedman, 1967). And a study of undergraduates in a predominantly black college and also in a surburban community college also found this pattern the most preferred by both men and women.

Actually, the early-interrupted pattern is probably the worst possible in terms of professional development. Havelock Ellis in his *Study of British Genius* noted that either very early marriage or fairly late marriage, or no marriage at all, was characteristic of achieving women. They thus "escaped from, or found a *modus vivendi* with, domestic and procreative claims." The early-interrupted pattern is contrary to all of these escapes. It interrupts the woman's career at a time when it is least stable, so that temporary defection is most serious; and when she herself still lacks the competence, aplomb, experience, and self-identity to cope with its costs.

Those who advocate or accept the early-interrupted pattern grant that some retooling or rust-removal may be required upon reentrance into the professional field, and a variety of programs have been instituted to supply it. For certain occupations this may be a suitable solution. But for those in the learned, scientific, or technical professions, it is not auspicious; this holds true regardless of sex. Speaking of the interruption of careers of men by military service, J. Douglas Brown noted that the losses were probably irreparable:

> It will never be possible to estimate accurately the number of creative scientists and engineers who were lost from the flow of trainees because of the interruptions and diversions of careers arising from World War II. Experience in organized military activity may contribute greatly to maturing a man's capacity in dealing with his fellows [just as, of course, marriage and motherhood may contribute to the maturing of a woman's]. It does not, however, offer an effective substitute for the exact, integrated, and continuous training afforded by a scientific or engineering program in a university or by intensive specialization in creative effort in industry. Interruption in the development of a scientist or research engineer, as with a medical doctor, appears to be costly in terms of quality and quantity of the end product. Too many men fail to return to their previous training programs or lose the momentum which carried them to the higher levels of attainment (Brown, 1954).

Women may lose their momentum also. Studies of the achievement motivation of women after graduation from college give equivocal results. One reported "a dramatic decrease in achievement motive [among 137 Radcliffe alumnae] between 5 and 10 years out of college" and attributed this "moratorium of achievement striving" to the assumption of family responsibilities during those years (Baruch, 1966, p. 102). But another study, of Jackson College graduates of the classes of 1953 and 1958, questioned five years after graduation and then again ten years after, found no such decline. In fact, this study found higher scores on achievement-striving among the older than among the younger subjects, suggesting an increase rather than a decline in the first decade after graduation (Eyde, 1968). Until we know more about the way motivations operate to lead women to re-enter active professional careers, little more can be said about how much reliance can be placed on its persistence.

Even if they do return, Alice Rossi, who very much disapproves of the early-interrupted pattern, points out, the years of greatest achievement potential have been lost. The early-interrupted pattern should not, she argues, be "widely or uncritically accepted until we have better answers to the question concerning the effect this withdrawal has upon the contributions we may expect from her. If we judge from the dozens of researches Harvey

Lehman has conducted on the relationship between age and achievement, the answer to this basic question must be a qualified 'not very much'" (Rossi, 1965, p. 102). This objection to the early-interrupted pattern on the basis of achievement has good research support. Lindsey P. Harmon, for example, studying the careers of science doctors, found "when the married women return to professional work they have returned to professional jobs that tend to be either teaching or research, but less frequently the balanced combination . . . characteristic of the men and of those women whose professional careers have been uninterrupted." This means, in effect, that they return "as an important reservoir for assistants and technicians and the less demanding professions, but only rarely for creative and original contributors to the more demanding professional fields" (Rossi, 1965, p. 107).

Ginzberg and his associates substantiated this criticism. They found that the achievement level of women with uninterrupted work histories was far below that of women with interrupted work histories, fewer than a third as many showing a high achievement level and five times as many showing a low achievement level (Table 9.1). It is quite possible that a selective bias was at work who continued their work despite the distractions of family obligations, while for the unmotivated, marriage and children may have been an acceptable excuse for low achievement. Equally likely as an explanation, however, is the fact that the women with uninterrupted work histories were single or childless. Since work history and family situation were themselves closely related, it is expectable that family situation was also related to achievement.

**Table 9.1** Achievement level of educated women by career patterns

| | Work history (in per cent) | |
|---|---|---|
| Achievement level | Continuous | Broken |
| High | 23 | 7 |
| Good | 41 | 10 |
| Medium | 29 | 47 |
| Low | 7 | 36 |
| Total | 100 | 100 |

Source: Eli Ginzberg et al., *Life Styles of Educated Women* (New York: Columbia University Press, 1966) p. 100.

The downward mobility characteristic of the early-interrupted pattern was demonstrated in a study of a less gifted population base on a representative national sample of 34,662 households. In this sample it was found that women originally in professional and technical occupations tended to return to clerical and sales positions, and women originally in clerical and sales positions to (nondomestic) service jobs. "This pattern of downward mobility . . . appears to be related to extensive periods of absence from the labor force. . ." (Shea, 1970, p. 171).

Criticisms of the early-interrupted career pattern in terms of achievement and downward mobility are basically from the point of view of the optimum utilization of human resources; they evaluate the pattern in terms of the loss it implies in creativity or achievement. They apply to men as well as to women. For many women, loss in achievement is more than compensated for by the satisfactions they derive from their domestic role; but such women are likely to be in the terminated career category rather than in an interrupted pattern.

Subtler and more relevant from the self-actualization point of view is Alice Rossi's argument against the early-interrupted pattern: that if a woman is enticed to withdraw from her career for a number of years, her husband and chldren will evolve a style of living dependent on her contribution as wife and mother. When she seeks to return to her work, far more reorientation and readjustment on everyone's part is called for than would have been if all had become accustomed to her role as an independent and active professional from the beginning.

### The late-interrupted patterns (B, C, D, E)

The late-interrupted patterns appeal to young women who are not in any hurry to undertake motherhood at an early age although, like the young women opting for the early-interrupted pattern, they might want the companionship of marriage at a fairly early age (D, E). In any event, after graduation or marriage they go right into professional or graduate training and practice, remaining with it for a long enough time to acquire self-confidence and to prove their mettle. Some might feel secure enough in their professional identities after five or six years; others might want to postpone motherhood ten or even fifteen years. In either case, by the time they do choose to have children they will be in a better position psychologically, socially, professionally, and even financially, to clear the hurdles.

There was a time when higher education and marriage for men as well as women (D, E) were held to be incompatible. Students were expelled if or when they married; but reversal of this policy took place, first for men and then also for women, especially at the graduate level. The merit of marriage under these auspices is that it is initiated in an atmosphere in which both partners are assumed to have the privilege of intellectual pursuits. Such a pattern, established early in a marriage, should have a good chance to continue later on in the nonacademic world outside.

Among women not even ready to make the commitment required in institutionalized marriage, let alone motherhood, the delayed marriage conducive to career facilitation is sometimes made possible by relationships that supply intimacy and companionship without demanding a permanent commitment. On the campuses of many universities, young men and women are finding suitable ways of relating to one another in which it is taken for granted by both that women have legitimate intellectual interests. Marriage may or may not result. Either way it makes possible a period of development toward autonomy on the part of young women, obviates premature marriage which might have a stunting effect, and makes for greater psychological independence. In such unions there is no need for the young woman to put the young man's career ahead of her own.

### Uninterrupted patterns (F, G, H)

Since marriage itself need offer no obstacle to either professional training or practice, and if neither marriage nor children intervenes, as in pattern H, the career pattern is also uninterrupted. Although statistical data on labor-force participation of women do not tell us the proportion of women who fall into these several patterns, it can be assumed that practically all of the small number of women who never marry follow uninterrupted patterns, and most of the married but childless women probably do also. In the Ginzberg sample, 91 percent of the single women followed the H pattern; and 83 percent of the married but childless women, pattern G.

Pattern F contemplates the possibility of marriage and children at a fairly early age, followed by professional training and uninterrupted practice thereafter. It is not a pattern that has received favorable consideration in the literature on career patterns for women for a number of reasons. Most thinking about careers has assumed a male model as standard; and there is a substantial research literature discouraging to a policy of early marriage.

In view of the assumptions against pattern F, it is difficult to make a persuasive case in its favor. But at least the data, however fragmentary, on which it rests deserve consideration. Two studies, one of women in social work, a profession sex-typed for women, and one of women with doctorates, showed that those who married and had their children before they received graduate or professional training were more likely to participate in the labor force on an uninterrupted basis than those who married after they had taken professional training (Astin, 1967; Tropman, 1968). It can be argued that only highly motivated women would have undertaken professional training after motherhood, so that a highly select population is involved. Still, even limiting the pattern to highly motivated women, it makes sense.

Another line of argument is more circuitous. It casts aside all assumptions based on male career patterns and tries to think solely in terms of the way young women develop. We noted above that young women find it impossible to make serious career plans until they know who their husbands are going to be, for everything depends on that crucial choice. Further, many also find it impossible to think seriously beyond having children. They may give a kind of vague nod in the direction of some kind of work later on in their lives, but they lack genuine conviction. Since they really cannot think seriously in terms of a career until the urgent marriage-and-motherhood imperatives have been met, it would seem to be the part of wisdom to go with rather than against this tide. We might think of the period of, say, 18 to 22 years as the "motherhood" stage in a young woman's life, a stage she would pass through and "outgrow" or "get over." Following this line of thinking, we would take it for granted that she had to get motherhood "out of her system" before she could plan beyond it. By the time she was about 25 she would be ready to resume her training wherever she had left off and continue uninterruptedly into her profession with fresh rather than dated preparation, with no need for re-tooling.

Certainly a caveat with respect to too-early marriage is in order. Too-youthful marriages tend to be less stable than later ones, but not less stable than those delayed too long. Alice Rossi (1965) emphasizes the loss of autonomy that young women experience when they marry young. Martinson (1955)concludes that young women tend to marry out of weakness rather than strength; and Hurley and Palonen (1967) advise against having children too early. Young marriages might require subsidies, perhaps in the form of long-term loans. Still, for many young women this timing of the two roles might prove optimal.

One of the pluses of this pattern has to do with the perspective in which it puts the lives of women. It accustoms us to see how small a part motherhood takes in the total life of a woman, how much in this day and age, it is a young woman's enterprise. It frees us to think of women in a wider context.

### Quasi interruptions: part-time work

When we spoke of the "one-and-a-half-role" pattern above, we referred to women who assigned a merely casual importance to their jobs. But there are some women to whom work would be a serious investment even if undertaken only on a part-time basis. Alice Rossi (1965) believes that under certain conditions, part-time employment may be a good solution for mitigating interruptions; Myrdal and Klein (1965) do not.

Part-time work may take several forms: part-time the year round or either part-time or full-time work during less than a full year. The second, except in the case of school teachers, is only a euphemism for seasonal unemployment, having the disadvantages of both part-time and full-time work. Usually what is meant by part-time work is anything less than the customary 40-hour week the year round.

The practical obstacles to the part-time solution for the problems involved in the uninterrupted pattern are considerable. The proportion of all women who have been part-time workers in one form or another has remained fairly constant for the last two decades. What the possibilities are for increasing the supply of such employment under existing conditions we do not know; that would depend on the willingness not only of women but also of employers. In 1969, the proportion of the female labor force employed in voluntary part-time work—as distinguished from those working part-time involuntarily and from those who wanted part-time work but were unemployed—varied by age, being lowest in the very years when children were youngest. In 1971, Committee W or the AAUP was recommending that part-time academic appointments for both women and men be institutionalized with all the privileges and prerogatives of full-time appointments, an ideal prototype solution for many.

The situation for professional women may not be as stringent as that for other women. They can arrange their schedules to take care of their maternal responsibilities; those who have special gifts may find it possible to paint, write, or practice at home.

### The two-career family

In the form of so-called "antinepotism" rules, there has been a strong opposition to two-career families in the United States. The teaming-up of husbands and wives has been discouraged. In France, however, legal provision is made to ensure that in the civil service, the teaching profession, and other careers, the husband or wife or a person already employed in a given district should have a certain priority for posts in the same area. In the assignment of personnel in the Soviet Union, the general rule, despite numerous exceptions, is that husbands and wives should not be separated. Not just a system of joint fellowships, but one, where practicable, of joint appointments (a system just the opposite to that represented by the antinepotism rules currently on the books), if not always enforceable, would help women in the pursuit of happiness. The idea is to think not in terms of separate, isolated individuals but in terms of an organic unit consisting of husband and wife, allowing for individualism or individuating as desired.

In the case of at least some women, finally, the integration of family and career is achieved in a relationship that is called the colleagueship. Where both husband and wife are in the same profession, they may operate as a team, or at least in tandem as they did under the domestic system of production. Such unions seem to be remarkably successful. In a study of women who competed for the 1942-43 Westinghouse Science Scholarship awards, it was found that "three out of five had husbands in the same or allied fields and were unanimous in stressing the support their husbands gave in their attempt to complete their advance training and remain in their fields after marriage. Two cases of colleagueship, one at Harvard University in the behavioral and social sciences, and one at California in biology, are presented in autobiographical detail in *Academic Women.* The going may still be rough even with a husband to offer support, but at least the split in the woman's life is reduced and the entire burden of her career is not placed on her shoulders alone. She does not have to pursue her happiness in a path 180 degrees apart from his.

Although the so-called "androgynous life" of wives and husbands in the two-career family has been greeted as the wave of the future (Bird, 1968), it should be noted that in such marriages, the wife's career is almost always subordinate to that of the husband. In one study of 53 such two-career families, the wife's career was viewed as merely a kind of hobby, an avocation rather than a vocation, in a substantial proportion with a traditional orientation. The women's primary role was defined as that of a wife rather than of a professional, and the husband was the status-giver and source of income. In some, the neotraditional, the wife's income was used and her profession was taken more seriously, but she still had sole responsibility for the children. Among those with an egalitarian orientation, some women deliberately kept their incomes down. Marriages in which the wife's income was greater than the husband's—labeled "matriarchal" by the researcher—were characterized by more problems than were the other three types (Paloma, 1970). The two-role ideology has a great deal to recommend it for helping women pursue happiness, but it is far from a guarantee of success.

The one clear and unequivocal conclusion that emerges from all the studies on the career patterns of women is that career pattern is not a simple or unidimensional variable; certainly the research so far has not located all the relevant variables or measured their impact convincingly. "Given the existing social arrangements," there does not seem to be any ideal way to reconcile the domestic functions assigned to women with the demands of their work roles as currently defined.

It is argued by some radical women that in view of the fact that we are going to need the services of professional women and are going to have to offer women attractive alternatives to motherhood, it is in the public interest as well as the interest of women themselves to take the career problems of women seriously, to make the careers of women as respectable and worthy as those of men, to see their career problems as amenable to rational solutions, to institutionalize them and hence render them predictable and assimilable. And so long as women seek careers, they should be permitted to run the course with a minimum of handicaps.

But while some women are insisting that career patterns of women be made as nearly like those of men as possible, there are others who are asking if this is not actually just one more illustration of sexism? Is this not accepting the male pattern as the standard against which to judge all patterns? Is this not taking for granted that the careers of men are *the* correct, proper, appropriate patterns for everyone? That the careers of all must follow the male pattern or be unacceptable? That the values implicit in achievement are the best values for everyone? Along with many others, including young male radicals, they ask if the game is worth the candle.

## IS THE GAME WORTH THE CANDLE?

The concept of career leads to the heart of one of the major upheavals we are undergoing today. It is tied up with the whole value-complex associated with achievement. Freud pointed out that we paid for civilization and its achievements with a sacrifice of personal gratifications; what men gave to their work was what they took from their families (Freud, 1958). And Talcott Parsons (1949) reminded us that in no sector of our society did "the dominant patterns stand in sharper contrast to those of the occupational world than in the family." Career success demands qualities that are precisely opposite to those demanded for family life. The work and family roles of men must therefore be kept strictly segregated lest one interfere with the other, and usually if there is a conflict it must be resolved in favor of the career. The payoff for this enormous investment in achievement by men in their occupational roles has been the enormous productivity of the economy. In this context, the powerful achievement drive implied in a career was functional. It might extort enormous costs from the individually driven men and their families, but it created affluence.

Young radicals in the 1960's were beginning to challenge the validity of this view. They looked around at their parents' generation and decided that the game of success—the rat race—was not worth the candle of human deprivation that it cost. Erik Grønseth, a Norwegian sociologist, concluded from a careful analysis of the ramifications of the occupational roles of men that although as now structured they might be functional for the status quo, they were nevertheless dysfunctional for society as a whole: "What is 'functional' for the short-term upkeep of a competitively, compensatory 'achievement'-oriented, 'open'-class social order, and for an integration based on this kind of 'achievement'-principle, may in the long run prove totally disintegrative" (Grønseth, 1970).

Disintegrative for marriage as well as for a whole society. We have quoted research evidence on the destructive effects on marriage of too-great role specialization. The emphasis there was on the wife's role, and the implication was that the wife should diversify her marital roles to make her life and her marriage more satisfying both to herself and to her husband.

But the implications for the husband's role are also pertinent. For a husband-father to be successful in the provider role he must invest enormous amounts of time in his work, time that could otherwise be devoted to his family. He must cultivate competitiveness, aggressiveness, rationality, calculation—traits, as Parsons has pointed out, not compatible with those required for happy ramily relationships. Thus (this study reported) the more successful the father was in his career, the less likely his marriage was to be successful. To avoid this result:

> The husband can simply hold back and not get overinvolved in his occupational pursuits. Recent work in occupational sociology indicates that this may in fact be occurring within certain middle class occupations, especially those in the large corporations. Frequently noted, in this regard, are the problems of middle management. At this level, the number of higher positions drops off precipitously and one of the adaptations to the strain inherent in the quest for promotion is simply to stop trying and transfer energies from the corporation to the family (Dizard, 1968, p. 79).

Philip Slater also raises questions about using the male concept of career, as it is now institutionalized, as the standard for either women or men. Perhaps, after all, it isn't that worthy of emulation. Perhaps male careers could also bear a bit of looking into. What would be wrong with a career pattern in which success does not demand the complete absorption the present male pattern does? For both men and women who preferred it?

In *Academic Women* it was pointed out that not all women were willing to invest this much of their lives in their careers; they did not want to put all their eggs in one basket. In a male context, such an attitude seems frivolous, lacking in seriousness. Now Philip Slater suggests that maybe these women were making more humane choices than the career-stricken men:

> "Career" is in itself a masculine concept (i.e., designed for males in our society). When we say "career" it connotes a demanding, rigorous, preordained life pattern, to whose goals everything else is ruthlessly subordinated—everything pleasurable, human, emotional, bodily, frivolous. It is a stern Calvinistic word. When a man asks a woman if she wants a career, it is intimidating. He is saying, are you willing to suppress half of your being as I am, neglect your family as I do, exploit personal relationships as I do, renounce all personal spontaneity as I do? Naturally she shudders a bit and shuffles back to the broom closet. She even feels a little sorry for him and bewails the unkind fate that has forced him against his will to become such a despicable person. The perennial success of this hoax perhaps contributes to the low opinion that men so often have of feminine intelligence (an opinion which, as any teacher knows, is otherwise utterly unfounded).
>
> A more effective (revolutionary, confronting) response would be to admit that a "career" thus defined, is indeed un-

desirable—that (now that you mention it) it seems like a pernicious activity for any human being to engage in, and should be eschewed by both men and women. Of course, she doesn't want a "career," nor do most humans, with the exceptions of a few males crazed, by childhood deprivation or Oedipal titillation, with insatiable desires for fame, power, or wealth. What she wants is a meaningful and stumulating activity, excitement, challenge, social satisfactions—all the things that middle-class males get from their jobs whether they are defined as "careers" or not. Rarely is she willing, however, to pay the price that masculine narcissism seduces men into paying in our society. She therefore accepts the definition of herself as the inferior sex, instead of adopting the revolutionary stance of the black militant ("black is beautiful"), and saying: "My unwillingness to sacrifice a host of human values to my personal narcissism and self-aggrandizement makes me the superior sex."

Such a stance would in fact liberate both sexes: Women would be freed from the suffocating stagnation of the artificial domestic role in which they have been imprisoned; men would be liberated from their enslavement to the empty promise (ever receding, always redefined as just out of reach, and unsatisfying even when grasped), of "success." Both could then live in a gratifying present, instead of an illusory future and an ill-remembered past (Slater, 1970).

Philip Slater is here shamelessly plagiarizing the ideas of Movement Women who propose to do precisely what he proposes: liberate both women and men from the crippling effects of artificial role constrictions. Adjusting the Establishment to the lives of women rather than the lives of women to the Establishment.

## REFERENCES

Astin, Helen S., "Personal and Environmental Factors Associated with the Participation of Women Doctorates in the Labor Force," (mimeographed, 1967).

Baruch, Rhoda, *The Achievement Motive in Women: A Study of the Implications for Career Development* (Unpublished doctoral dissertation, Harvard, 1966), p. 102.

———, *The Interruption and Resumption of Women's Careers* (Harvard Studies in Career Development, No. 60, 1966).

Bernard, Jessie, unpublished study of students at the Federal City College, Washington, D. C., and Montgomery Junior College, Bethesda, Md.

———, *Academic Women* (University Park: Pennsylvania State University Press, 1964).

Bird, Caroline, *Born Female, The High Cost of Keeping Women Down* (New York: McKay, 1968), Chapter 8.

Brown, J. Douglas, "Meeting Requirements for Scientific, Engineering, and Managerial Manpower," in William Haber et al. (eds.), *Manpower in the United States: Problems and Policies* (New York: Harper, 1954), p. 194.

Dizard, Jan, *Social Change in the Family* (Chicago: Community and Family Study Center, University of Chicago, 1968), p. 79.

Eyde, Lorraine D., "Work Motivation of College Alumnae: Five-Year Followup," *Jour. Counseling Psych.*, 15 (March 1968), 199-202.

Freedman, Mervin, *The College Experience* (San Francisco: Jossey-Bass, 1967), Chapter 10.

Freud, Sigmund, *Civilization and Its Discontents* (Garden City, N.Y.: Doubleday-Anchor, 1958), pp. 50-51.

Garfinkle, Stuart, "Work in the Lives of Women," paper prepared for International Union for the Scientific Study of Population, London, 1969, p. 5.

Ginzberg, Eli, et al., *Life Styles of Educated Women* (New York: Columbia University Press, 1966).

Grønseth, Erik, "The Dysfunctionality of the Husband Provider Role in Industrialized Societies," paper prepared for the 7th World Congress of Sociology, Varna, 1970.

Harmon, Lindsey P., *Profiles of the Ph.D.'s in the Sciences,* NAS-NRC pub. no. 1292 (1965), p. 61.

Hurley, John R., and Donna P. Palonen, "Marital Satisfaction and Child Density among University Student Parents," *Jour. Mar. and Fam.*, 29 (Aug. 1967), 483-484.

Martinson, Floyd M., "Ego Deficiency as a Factor in Marriage," *Amer. Sociol. Rev.*, 20 (April 1955), 161-164.

Myrdal, Alva, and Viola Klein, *Women's Two Roles* (London: Routledge and Kegan Paul, 1956), p. 162.

Paloma, Margaret M., "The Myth of the Egalitarian Family: Familial Roles and the Professionally Employed Wife," paper prepared for meetings of American Sociological Association (Aug. 1970).

Parsons, Talcott, "The Social Structure of the Family," in Ruth Nanda Anshen (ed.), *The Family; Its Function and Destiny* (New York: Harper, 1949), p. 262.

Rossi, Alice, "Barriers to the Career Choice of Engineering, Medicine, or Science among American Women," in Jacqueline A. Mattfield and Carol G. Van Aken (eds.), *Women and the Scientific Professions* (Cambridge: M.I.T. Press, 1965).

Shea, John R., et al., *Dual Careers: A Longitudinal Study of Labor Market Experience of Women,* vol. 1 (Columbus: Center for Human Resources Research, Ohio State University, 1970), p. 171.

Slater, Philip E., "What Hath Spock Wrought?—Freed Children, Chained Mothers," in *The Pursuit of Loneliness, American Culture at the Breaking Point* (Boston: Beacon Press, 1970), reproduced in *Washington Post,* March 1, 1970.

Tropman, John E., "The Married Professional Social Worker," *Jour. Mar. and Fam.,* 30 (Nov. 1968), 661-665.

## SUGGESTED READINGS

Jessie Bernard, *The Future of Marriage.* New York: World Book, 1972. Demonstrates that marriage is much more destructive of women than men, and makes proposals for change.

Cynthia Fuchs Epstein, *Woman's Place,* Berkeley, Ca.: Univ. of California Press, 1970. A good companion to this Bernard essay in that it describes why the professional woman apparently underperforms, underachieves, and under produces.

Constantina Safilios-Rothschild (editor), *Toward a Sociology of Women,* Lexington, Ky.: Xerox College Publishing, 1972. A collection of research studies on women who work, with special focus on change in traditional sex roles.

ABCDEFGH79876543